FIRST CLASS

a child's first lessons in knowing God

TnT Ministries

CHRISTIAN FOCUS PUBLICATIONS

TnT Ministries (which stands for Teaching and Training) was launched in February 1993 by Christians from a broad variety of denominational backgrounds who are concerned that teaching the Bible to children be taken seriously. They have been in charge of the Sunday School of 50 teachers at St Helen's Bishopsgate, an evangelical church in the City of London, for nine years, during which time a range of Biblical teaching materials has been developed. TnT Ministries also runs training days for Sunday School Teachers.

First Class

TnT Ministries
29 Buxton Gardens
Acton
London W3 9LE
Tel: 0181 992 0450

Published in 1997 by Christian Focus Publications Ltd.
Geanies House, Fearn, Tain
Ross-shire IV20 1TW
Tel: 01862 871 541; Fax: 01862 871 699

This book and others in the TnT range can be purchased from your local Christian bookshop. Alternatively you can write to TnT Ministries or place your order with the publisher.

ISBN: 1-85792-224-7

Cover designed by Douglas McConnach
Printed and bound in Great Britain by Cromwell Press

All Scripture references are from the Good News Bible except where indicated.

Contents

Term 1

Term 2

The Christmas Story

FIRST CLASS

a child's first lessons in knowing God

First Class is a series of lessons designed to introduce small children to basic concepts about God and his world. The lessons can be used at home, or in a class, and are appropriate for children aged between 2 and 3. It comprises 34 lessons, during the course of which the child is taught about the God who made everything, even them, and who loves them and knows all about them. A further 3 lessons are for use at Christmas and teach the child the basic facts of the Christmas story.

First Class can be used anywhere where there are 2-3 year old children – a creche, a playgroup or at home – and is good preparation for children prior to their entering the church Sunday School. It can be taught by parents or anyone else who has the care of young children, and no special teacher training is required.

Why teach 2-3 year old children?

Children of this age have already demonstrated their remarkable capacity to learn. They can identify their favourite characters in story books and on TV, eg Postman Pat and Fireman Sam, and are able to respond to simple instructions, eg 'please pick up that toy', or 'come and have a drink'. They respond emotionally to people and stories, and are able to enjoy loving relationships with parents and other significant adults. They also have the ability to develop a simple trust in God.

It is in this area that we hope **First Class** will help. A little girl of nearly 2 ½ , following the lesson on 'God made the earth', saw a bowl of flowers, picked one out, sniffed it, gave it to her mother and said, "Jesus made that". Do not underestimate the capacity of small children to respond in simple faith to the God who made them and loves them.

At this age, children are most receptive, so we should use the opportunity to teach them about God carefully, and in a way which will provide a foundation for them to grow into maturity in Christ in later years.

How do young children learn?

A typical 2-3 year old is still developing large physical movements, such as running and jumping. They have a limited vocabulary and love to practise skills by repeating words or phrases. They mainly learn by repetition.

Especial care needs to be taken over the language you use with children of this age. Adults have a way of complicating talk about God with long words. For children, words should be simple and sentances short. DO NOT USE CHRISTIAN JARGON: e.g. sin; a young child will understand "all the naughty things I do."

Visually, children of this age love bright colours and simple images. Therefore, pictures used in teaching sessions must be big, clearly drawn and uncluttered. Hand/eye co-ordination is at an early stage, so colouring in tends to come out a scribble. Even though the end results can look disastrous, they still enjoy it and can take pride in what they have created. They cannot use scissors, but are able to glue with help.

Children enjoy making things to keep or take home that remind them of what has been learned, even if they have had very little part in their making. Therefore much of the craft-work outlined in the lessons needs to be prepared in advance of the time when you are teaching the children in class.

A 2-3 year old child has a very short attention span (3-5 minutes maximum) and the lessons are designed with this in mind. It is, therefore, important to pick a suitable time for the teaching – with very young children who take time to settle down it may be better to wait until after their refreshments. Children of this age should be taught in small groups, (we suggest 6 maximum, but preferably 4) so that each child can be involved, Opportunities for reinforcing the lesson should be found during play time.

How to use it

We have tried to design the lessons so that they can be used either at home, or as a short slot in a longer session. If it is part of a creche during church, then it would be ideal to fit in after the children have settled down and had time to play. The lesson can be taught as an interlude in a middle or end of a playgroup, or very naturally at home on a Sunday afternoon or other convenient time of the week. It is good to try and be consistent with the children, teaching a lesson each week, so that the ideas build on each other in the child's mind.

Each lesson is set out in the same way. The title is followed by the **lesson aim,** which details what the child is expected to learn from that particular session. This is followed by a section entitled **Teacher Preparation**, which sets out a Biblical foundation for the lesson. This bit is easy to skip, but for the sake of the children and for yourself, please be committed to making adequate spiritual preparation, as well as preparing the visual aids etc. Imparting spiritual knowledge, especially to those with little discernment of truth like children, is a job that God takes very seriously indeed. Even though it seems simple and straightforward, you need to spend time praying for the children and thinking through the truth you are trying to impart, so that God the Holy Spirit will bless the work. You may well find that your own walk with God is enriched in the process!

The next section consists of a detailed **lesson plan,** which must be thoroughly understood and learnt, so that the child can be taught without reference to the lesson material. The lesson finishes with ideas for craft work, games , songs, etc and suggestions for how the lesson can be reinforced at home.

Give time to teaching the children, letting them contribute or ask questions, but keep it as short as possible, otherwise attention will wander and the opportunity will be lost. Try to strike a balance between the lesson being fun, and yet serious. Your attitude is very important — they will take the lead from you.

Remember to always check activities and crafts for potential **Safety** problems.Although every care has been taken in the preparation of this material to avoid safety hazards, you need to be aware of possible problems in the environment or from the children. 3 year olds can be very boistrous!

Each lesson ends with a **Prayer.** Although we often find the idea of prayer difficult to understand, for children it is often very natural. Closing eyes and holding hands together is not necessary, but it helps them to concentrate. Try to get them to understand that God is listening, and wants to hear our prayers

Home Reinforcement is vital, and we must never forget that parental input is the main influence in a young child's life; the creche/ playgroup can only reinforce what goes on in the home. It is therefore helpful to establish contact with the parents and try to get them to follow up the lesson with the child. Feel free to duplicate the Reinforcement section and give it to the parents.

Some of the home reinforcement ideas may seem a little repetitious. Children learn by repetition at this age. Try to make it personal, however, by using the prayer at night with them for example. This will help the child to understand the lesson, rather than to just repeat it.

What results?

We believe that, carefully and prayerfully used, these lessons can be very important for a child's first steps in knowing God through Jesus. We would hope that **First Class** will result in:

1. The child developing a simple trust in God.
2. The parents learning to be relaxed, natural and confident in teaching their child about God
3. The child entering Sunday School ready to learn and take part in a more traditional lesson.
4. The teacher growing in their own relationship with God. You cannot teach even a 2-3 year old something you do not fully understand.

Teaching 2-3 year old children is an important job and is worth doing well, even though it is time-comsuming if done properly. Jesus said: "Let the little children come to me, and do not hinder them, for the kingdom of God belongs to such as these". (Luke 18v16). If Jesus thought children important, who are we to deny them access to his word which brings life?

TnT Ministries

Thank you, God, for my hands

Lesson aim: to know that God made me

Preparation

1. Read Psalm 139: 1-18
2. Answer the following questions:
   - what does God know about my thoughts?
     my words?
     my actions?
   - did God have anything to do with my conception and development within the womb?
   - what control does God have over my life span?
3. Think for a while about the wonder of God's intimate knowledge of each one of us, and of the children you will be teaching.
4. Pray for each child you teach, remembering that God made them and knows them intimately.
5. Choose and prepare visual aids.

Show children your hands, using appropriate comments,

- what are these called? these are my hands!
- who can say "hands"? (get them to repeat the word)
- Ask children to hold out their own hands in turn.Then the group can say 'those are Charlie's hands', 'Rachel's hands...' etc.
- Count fingers.
- Wiggle fingers.

What can we do with our hands? If the children will not volunteer things we can do, go through a list of things, demonstrating each action:

- hold (cuddly toy) ▪ pick up ▪ eat with ▪ draw with ▪ stroke, pat (animals, pets, cuddly toys) ▪ catch and throw (they will do this badly!) ▪ do up buttons, get dressed ▪ clap ▪ push ▪ beckon, point ▪ hold hands ▪ tickle

Who made our hands?

Tell the children that God made our hands.
Comment on how wonderful are our hands and how we should say thank you to God for making our hands.

Prayer

Thank you, God, for making my hands. Amen.

Visual aids

hands, things to demonstrate actions mentioned in lesson.

Activities

1. Ask child to place hand on sheet of plain paper. Draw round child's hand. Write child's name and "thank you, God, for my hands" on the paper. Let them take it home.
2. Finger painting (very messy - only at home, or if you have enough time to clean up afterwards
3. Teach this activity rhyme (based on "Tommy Thumb")

   Tommy Thumb, Tommy Thumb,
   who made you?
   God made me, God made me,
   how do you do.

   Then repeat for each finger:
   1st Finger: Peter Pointer...
   2nd Finger: Middle Man...
   3rd Finger: Ruby Ring...
   Little Finger: Baby Small...

4. Teacher puts hands behind back. "Where are my hands?"
   - Bring hands out - "Who made my hands?" "Who made your hands?"
5. Using a collection of dolls and soft toys, count the hands. Only count those with fingers. Separate toys with hands from those without.

Reinforcement

1. Ask child to perform simple tasks, eg open and shut door, pick up items, turn pages of book. Each time ask, "Who made your hands?"
2. Bathtime. Wash hands, splash, hold water in cupped hands, Ask, "Who made your hands?"
3. Draw round hands on coloured paper, cut out and stick them on a cupboard or notice board. Do the entire family. Ask child to identify the hands, eg Daddy's hands, Ask, "Who made Daddy's hands?"etc.

Term 1 Lesson 2

Thank you, God, for my feet

Lesson aim: to know that God made me

Preparation

1. Read Psalm 37:30-31; 40:1-3; 119:105; 2 John: 6. (NIV)
2. Answer the following questions:
   - walking in the Bible often denotes the direction of our lives. What are the two choices we have? - see Proverbs 1:15-16; 9:6
   - How do we know which is the right way to go?
   - How do we keep our feet from slipping?
3. Think about the importance of studying God's word, and how this helps us to avoid falling into sin.
4. Pray for each child,asking God to help you teach his word clearly.
5. Choose appropriate visual aids.

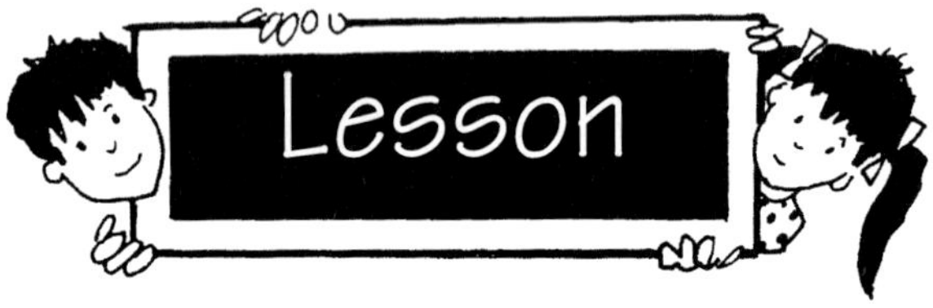

- Sit everyone down on the floor in a circle with feet pointing inwards. Ask children to tell you what their feet are called?
- Point to a child's foot. "Whose foot is this?" "This is Jack's foot".

What can we do with our feet?

Get children to demonstrate:

- walking
- stamping like a giant
- running
- kicking a ball
- jumping
- standing on one leg
- dancing to music

Ask them: "Who made our feet?"
God made our feet
Comment on how wonderful are our feet.
We must thank God for our feet.

Prayer

Thank you, God, for making our feet. Amen.

Visual Aids

feet, ball, appropriate music to dance

Activities

1. Dancing games, eg Hokey-cokey
   Here we go round the mulberry bush
   The Grand Old Duke of York
2. Have a collection of funny shoes/slippers to dress up in (do keep track of which child owns which pair of shoes.)
3. Draw round each child's feet (wearing shoes). Cut out and make into a collage. Name each foot.

Reinforcement

1. Ask child to perform simple actions. eg Go and get a toy; run round the room; etc Each time ask - "Who made your feet?" "How did you move?"
2. Bath time - count toes, wiggle toes, kick, wash feet. Ask, "Who made your feet?"
3. Play this little piggy went to market. Ask, "Who made your feet?"
4. Trace child's foot onto coloured sugar paper, cut out and stick up on board or cupboard. Do the same for the entire family. Ask child to identify the feet. "Whose feet are those?" "Those are Daddy's feet." "Who made Daddy's feet?" etc.
5. Lie on the floor and wave feet in the air. "Who made my feet?" "Who made your feet?"
6. Practice jumping. See how far child can jump. "Who made your feet?"

Term 1 Lesson 3

Thank you, God, for my eyes

Lesson aim: to understand how wonderful are the eyes that God has given us

Preparation

1. Read Psalm 94:9, Proverbs 15:3, Matthew 6:22-23.
2. Answer the following questions:
   - who made my eyes?
   - what does it mean - that "God can see"?
   - why should this affect the kind of lives we live?
   - does it matter what we watch?
3. Think about the effect your life has on the children you teach. What sort of example are you?
4. Pray for each child you are teaching, that they will come to know the God who made them.
5. Choose appropriate visual aids and activities.

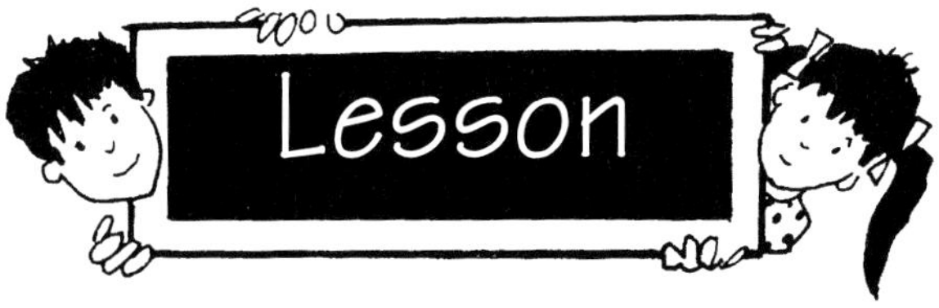

- Ask: "Where are my eyes? Where are your eyes?"
- Show pictures of animals, birds, fish, people - ask the children to point to the eyes.
- Tell children that all of them have eyes so that they know where they are going.
- Talk about why we need our eyes - to find our breakfast, cross the road, see Mummy and Daddy when they come into the room, find our toys, see the beautiful things around us, eg flowers, birds.
- The children can close their eyes and try and pick up something from the table.
- Our eyes are wonderful, we must thank God for our eyes.

Prayer

Thank you, God, for making my eyes. Amen.

Visual aids

Pictures of animals, birds, fish and people with eyes that are clear to see. Things that are good to look at, eg flowers, models/pictures of animals, lovely scenery,etc.

Activities

1. Face with moving eyes.
   Photocopy pages10 and 11 back to back for each child.Prior to the lesson cut out eye holes, cut off strip with irises, cut off strips a and b. Follow instructions on back of sheet.
   Children colour face, then insert eye strip. Strip can be moved to make eyes look left and right.
2. Make masks with eye holes. Children decorate masks with gummed paper shapes and glitter pens.
3. Play 'I Spy'. "Who can see something green?" etc. Anything that is the correct colour is a right answer. (Or, who can see a fish?)
4. Play hide and seek, either for a person or an object.

Reinforcement

1. Hold child's hand and turn out the light. Can they see anything? Turn light back on. "Who made my eyes?" The same can be done by covering each eye in turn.
2. Ask child to point out eyes on their soft toys/dolls and in picture books.
3. Ask child to choose a toy, etc. "How did you know where to go?" "How did you know which one to choose?" "Who made your eyes?" This can also be used to reinforce previous lessons on hands and feet.
4. Blow up a balloon and pat it round the room with child helping. "How do you know where the balloon is?" "Who made your eyes?"
5. Place a small object under a cup. "Can you see it?" "How do you know it is there?" "Who made your eyes?"
6. Blind man's buff. An adult will need to be the one who is blindfolded. "Who made your eyes?"
7. Look at a picture book together. "Who made your eyes?"

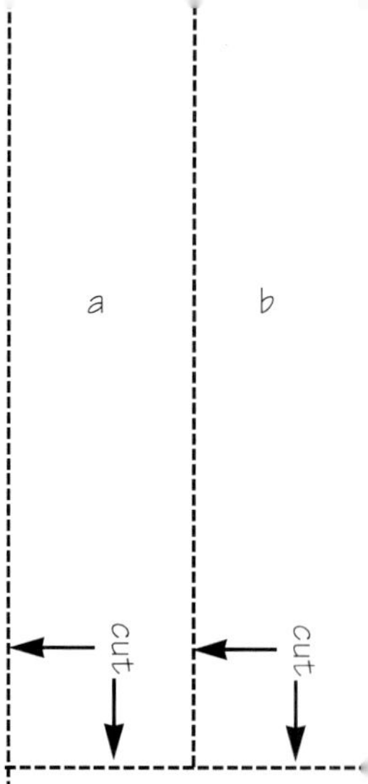

Thank you, God, for my eyes

stick 'b' to
shaded area

stick 'a' to
shaded area

Slip 'c' under retaining straps 'a' and 'b'.
Move from side to side to move eyes .

c

Term 1 Lesson 4

Thank you, God, For my ears

Lesson aim: to understand how useful are the ears God has given us.

Preparation

1. Read 2 Kings 19:16,
   Nehemiah 1:6,
   Job 42:4-6,
   Romans 10:14, Psalm 94:9.
2. Answer the following questions:
   - what does it mean that "God can hear"?
   - why is this important?
   - can we have a relationship with God if we have never heard about him?
3. Think about the children's need to hear about God. How can you teach them about God in a way they can understand?
4. Pray for each child you teach, remembering their need to hear God's word if they are to become his children.
5. Choose appropriate visual aids

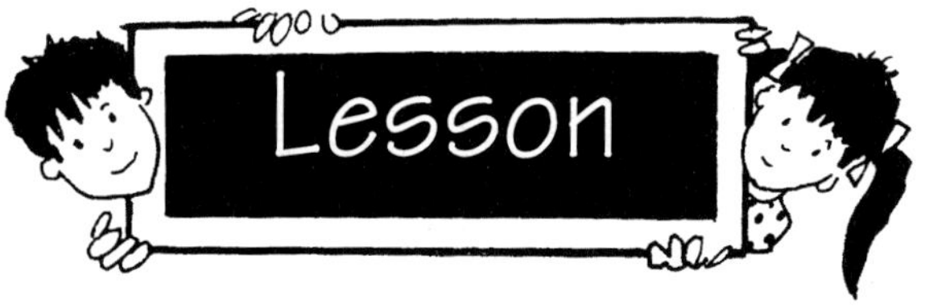

- Ask the children, Where are my ears? Where are your ears?
- Show pictures of animals and people with as many differently shaped ears as you can find.
- Ask the children to point to the ears on each head.
- Talk about why we need ears - to hear Daddy and Mummy, to listen to singing, birds, music, trains, planes, cars, etc
- Make a tape with different sound for the children to identify: dog bark, cat miaow, door closing, balloon popping etc.
- Speak loudly, then in a whisper. We can hear loud things and quiet things
- "Who made your ears?" "God made your ears". We must thank God for our ears.

Prayer

Thank you, God, for making my ears. Amen.

Visual aids

- Pictures of animals and people with different shaped ears.
- A tape of various sounds and cassette recorder.
- Musical instruments, rattles, whistles, etc.
- Pot of dried beans.
- Scour your house for things that make funny noises - Crackly paper, etc.

Activities

1. Make a head band from coloured sugar paper or card. Write "Thank you God, for my ears" on it. Have cut outs of big ears in card for children to choose. Glue or staple ears onto head band.
2. Play musical bumps. Reinforce by asking, "Who made your ears?"
3. Have 4 big pictures - a sheep, a cow, a duck, a pig. Pin each picture up in different parts of the room, eg ducks in one corner, pig in another corner, etc. Tell children you are the farmer and they are the animals. When you make the appropriate noise they are to run to the animal whose noise you are making. Ask each time, "Who made your ears?"

Reinforcement

1. Ask child to point out which of their toys have ears. Look at the different shapes. Ask child to point to his/her ears. Ask, "Who made your ears?"
2. Send child out of the room to wait till you call. Ask, "Who made your ears?". This can be repeated using different sounds.
3. Ask a friend to speak to the child on the telephone."Who made your ears?"
4. Go for a walk and see how many different sounds you can identify. "Who made your ears?"

Term 1 Lesson 5

Thank you, God, for my nose

Lesson aim: to know that God made our noses

Preparation

1. Read Genesis 1 v26-27, 1Corinthians 12 v14-20, Psalm 139 v13-16.
2. Answer the following questions:-
   - how did God make man?
   - how does man differ from the animals?
   - are some parts of the body more important than others?
   - why is it important to know that God is responsible for the way I am made?
3. Think about all the good things we would miss if we did not have noses. How does our sense of smell help us to stay safe?
4. Pray for each child you teach, asking God to help you explain to the children the wonder of his creating them.
5. Choose appropriate visual aids.

- Point to your nose. Ask, "What is this called?" "This is my nose".
- "Who can say, nose?"
- "Point to your nose".
- Discuss what a nose is for - breathing, smelling. Look at pictures of different sorts of noses. Get children to point to the noses. Talk about why the noses vary (use of nose to find food, etc.).
- Give children various things to smell, eg perfume, an onion, a flower, .
- Ask, "Who made your nose?" "God made your nose". – We must thank God for our noses.

Prayer

Thank you, God, for my nose. Amen.

Visual aids

- Pictures of different types of nose – animal and human
- Objects with a distinctive smell.

Activities

1. **Make a flower.** Each child requires 1 small paper plate, 1 garden stick, 10 paper petals
   Prior to lesson write "thank you, God, for my nose" in the middle of the paper plate. Attach a garden stick to the back of the plate using sellotape. Allowing 1 ¼ A4 sheets coloured paper per child, cut out petals, (Each sheet is folded into 8). Put 10 petals into an envelope for each child. Children glue petals around rim of plate.

   - When circle of petals is completed, place a drop of perfume in the centre of the plate for children to smell.
   - Ask "Who made your nose?"
2. Play a game with the objects used in the lesson. Who can identify the different smells? Ask "Who made your nose?"
3. Ask children to breathe in in unison, then breathe out making a noise. Ask, "Who made your nose?"

Reinforcement

1. When preparing food allow child to smell different things you use, as well as food cooking. Ask, "Who made your nose?"
2. Go for a walk and see how many different smells you can identify. Ask "Who made your nose?"
3. Demonstrate blowing your nose. Help child blow his/her nose. Ask "Who made your nose?"
4. Watch an animal (especially a dog) using its nose to find things. Ask, "Who made noses?"

Term 1 Lesson 6

Thank you,God, for my mouth

Lesson aim: to know that God made my mouth

Preparation

1. Read Exodus 4:10-17, Psalm 119:9-16, Matthew 15:1-20, James 3:9-10.
2. Answer the following questions:
   - who made my mouth?
   - is what comes out of my mouth important?
   - how do I treat God's word?
   - why did Jesus condemn the Pharisees and teachers of the Law in Matthew 15:1-20?
   - why must I control my tongue?
3. Think about the power of words, and especially of the power of God's word to revive those who hear it.
4. Pray for each child you teach, asking God to help you speak clearly so that they will understand more about him.
5. Choose appropriate visual aids.

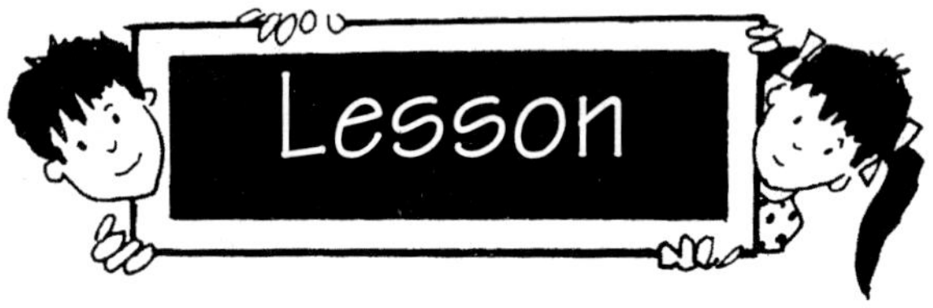

- Ask the children to point to their mouths. What do we do with our mouths?:
  - eat and drink ▪ speak ▪ sing ▪ call out loudly
  - whisper ▪ make animal noises

  Get children to repeat the actions after you. (Have smarties or pieces of bread for them to eat.)
  - Who can open their mouth really wide?
  - Who can smile/look sad,etc.

  Talk to children about how they would manage without a mouth:
  - no food will go into a closed mouth
  - get child to try and talk with mouth closed
  - how do we know someone is happy if they do not smile?
- Ask: "Who made your mouth?"
  God made your mouth.
  We must thank God for our mouths.

Prayer

Thank you, God, for my mouth. Amen.

Visual aids

Smarties, bread roll.

Activities

1.Make a 'mouth' to put things into.Each chid requires:
   - a yoghurt pot
   - 1 circle of material large enough to go over the top of the pot
   - 1 rectangle of paper with "thank you, God, for my mouth" written on it.
   - a few smarties

   a) Cut a slit for a mouth in the circle of material
   b) Place material over top of yogurt pot and secure with sellotape (child holds material, adult sellotapes).
   c) Glue rectangle of paper around yoghurt pot.
   d) Put smarties into pot through 'mouth'.
2. Sing some nursery rhymes or simple choruses - ask: "Who made your mouth?"
3. Play a chasing game, with the chasers pretending to be lions roaring (beware of children being frightened)

Reinforcement

1. Meal times - after having something nice to eat ask, "Who made your mouth?"
2. Ask child to open his/her mouth wide. Adult draws what is inside - tongue, teeth, lips. Talk about why we need a tongue, teeth, lips etc.Ask, "Who made your mouth?"
3. Make different sounds with your mouth. Ask,"Where did that sound come from?" Get child to copy sound if he/she can."Who made your mouth?"
4. Look at different sorts of mouths in a picture book - beak, crocodile,etc. "Who made mouths?"
5. Have a collection of items and get child to separate into edible and non-edible. Talk about why things are inedible "Who made your mouth?"
6. Demonstrate use of toothbrush. Talk about importance of keeping teeth clean. "Who made your mouth?"
7. Play a game with the family. Sit round in a circle. Everyone takes turns in saying their names. First time round do it in a whisper, then normal volume, then in a shout. "Who made your mouth?"

Term 1 Lesson 7

Thank you, God, for my family

Lesson aim: to understand that God has put us in families

Preparation

1. Read Genesis 2:18,
   Exodus 1:21,
   Psalm 68:4-6,
   Mark 3:33-35
2. Answer the following questions:-
   - is it good for a person to be on their own with no family?
   - how did the Israelites see the family?
   - how do we become part of God's family?
3. Think about the importance of family life. Are there any children you teach who come from single parent families?
4. Pray for each child you teach, asking God for wisdom to deal with any children who may not have both parents at home.
5. Choose appropriate visual aids.

- It is important to be aware of the family background of the children you teach, and to be sensitive in your teaching.
- Show children pictures of different families, eg pigs, ducks, cats, people. Ask them to point to the parent(s) and the children. Have pictures of a granny and grandpa as well as a father, mother and children. Tell the children that the parents/grandparents and children are called a family.
- What are families for?
  - Grown ups - look after me
  - feed me
  - dress me
  - comfort me, etc
  - brothers and sisters - play with me
  - help me, etc
- Remember - small children are usually totally egocentric. Tell children God has given us our families.
- We must thank God for our families.

Prayer

Thank you, God, for my family. Amen.

Visual aids

Pictures of different types of animal and human families. Pictures of adults or older children doing things with a small child.

Activities

1. Give each child a sheet of paper with "Thank you, God, for my family" written on it. Cut out pictures from magazines of grannies, grandpas, mothers, fathers, children, babies, animals.
   - Ask child to choose appropriate pictures to make up their family,
   - Child glues them onto sheet of paper.
2. Have a selection of toys that can be sorted into families, eg Sylvanian families. Get children to separate them into families. Ask "Who made your family?"
3. Play at families. Let children be the mummy, daddy, children, grandparents, etc and have a tea party or similar.

Reinforcement

1. Look through photographs of the family, extended as well as nuclear. Remind child that God gave us our family.
2. Happy families card game for older children. For younger children spread the cards out and sort out which families go together.
3. Sort out soft toys into "families" - eg pigs, bears, monkeys.
4. Talk about their friends' families. "Who belongs to Andrew's family?" "Does he have a sister?" etc.
5. Sit the family down together. All close their eyes and one member leaves the room. Ask child who is missing. Remind child, God gave us our family.

Term 1 Lesson 8

Jesus loves little children

Lesson aim: to teach each child that Jesus loves him/her

Teacher Preparation

1. Read Luke 18:15-17, Matthew 18:1-6.
2. Answer the following questions:
   - why did the disciples rebuke people for bringing their children to Jesus?
   - what does it mean to receive the kingdom of God like a little child?
   - how does God view a person who causes a child to sin?
3. Think about the fact that God loves each child you teach. Is there anything in your life that will prevent any of them coming to Jesus?
4. Pray for each child you teach, remembering that God loves each one.
5. Choose appropriate visual aids.

- Remind children that God made them.
- Remind them that Jesus is God.
- Tell story from Luke 18:15-17, using pictures from a child's story Bible.
- Show pictures of lots of different children.
- Tell them that Jesus loves all these children.
- Get children to point to themselves and say,"Jesus loves me".

Prayer

Thank you, Jesus, for loving me. Amen.

Visual aids

- Child's Story Bible
- Pictures of different children.

Activities

1. Make a dancing children crown.
   - Photocopy sheets 17 and 18 onto card, 1 set for each child.
   - Prior to lesson, cut off left side and top portion of each sheet as indicated, cutting around thick black line and hand of left child.
   - Children colour both sheets.
   - Glue one sheet to the other sheet with cut off left side of sheet B on top of right side of sheet A (see diagram). Do the same with the remaining 2 ends so that children are in a circle facing outwards.

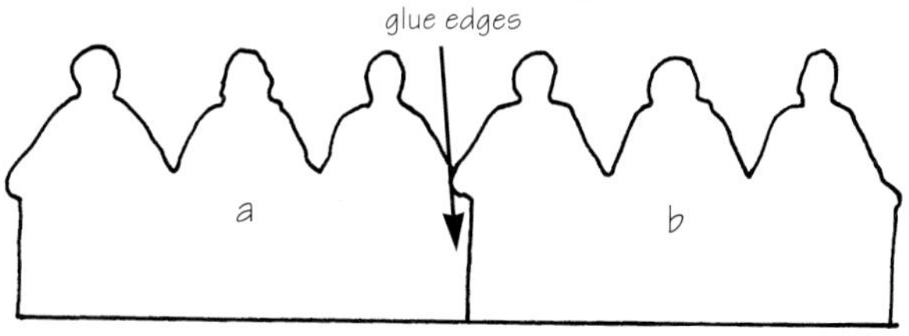

2. Sit children in a circle facing inwards. Take 1 child by the hand and walk round the outside of the circle saying "Jesus loves little children. Jesus loves 'N'. ('N' is the name of the child you come to). With each word child pats the top of the head of the next child in the circle. At 'N', child doing the patting changes place with 'N'. The sentences are repeated until each child has had a go.

Reinforcement

1. Use times when you hug/cuddle children to tell child that you love him/her and God also loves him/her,"even more than Mummy /Daddy does."
2. Find pictures of children in magazines, cut them out and let child glue them onto a big piece of paper to make a collage. Ask "Who loves little children?"

cut
cut
Jesus loves little children

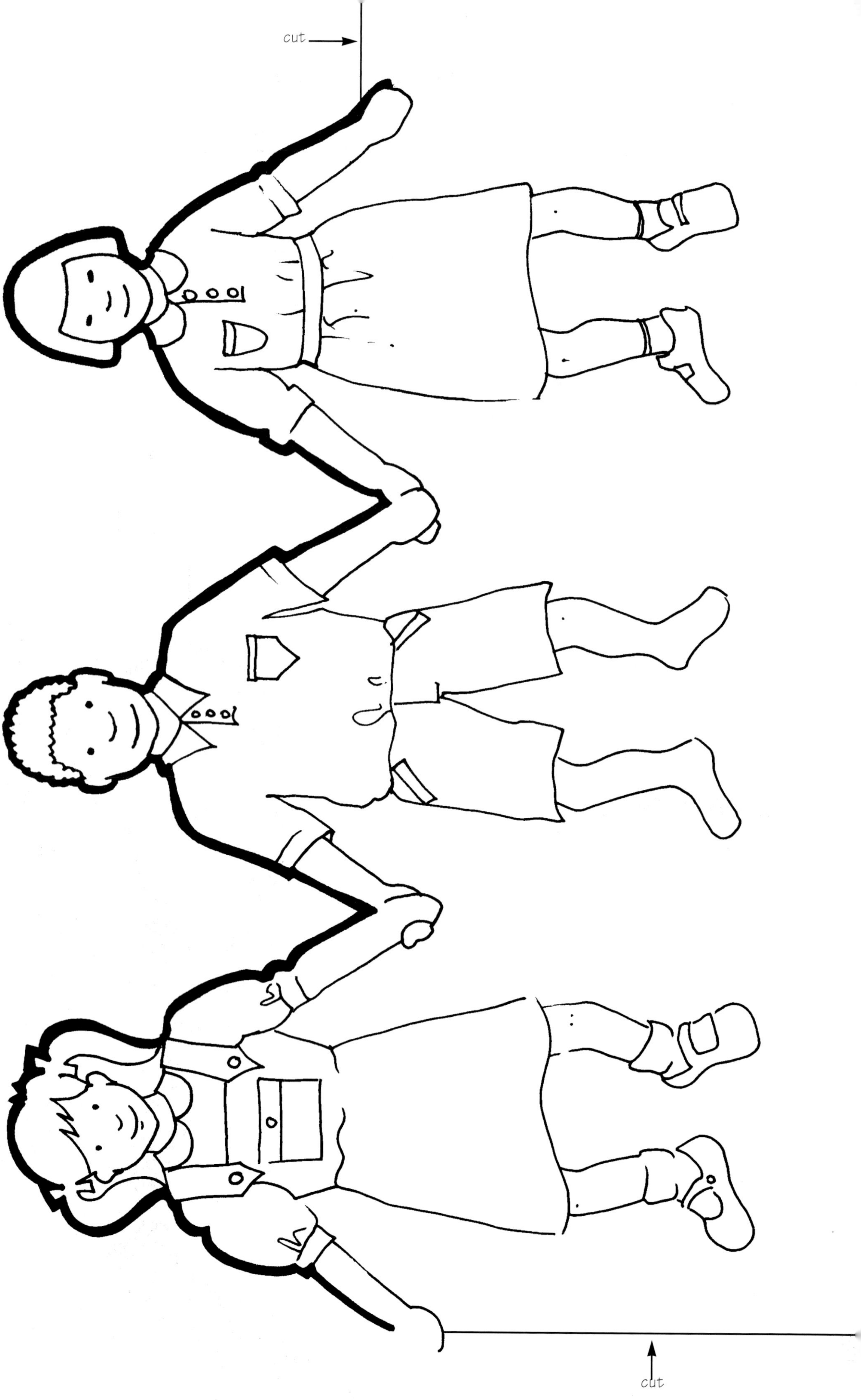
cut
cut

Term 1 Lesson 9

Jesus walks on the water

Lesson aim: to teach that Jesus is God

Teacher Preparation

1. Read Matthew 14:22-33, Mark 6:45-52, John 6:15-21.
2. Answer the following questions:-
   - where was Jesus when the disciples set off in the boat?
   - when the disciples saw Jesus walking on the water, what did they think he was?
   - how do we know that the boat wasn't close enough to shore for Jesus to be paddling?
3. Think about how the disciples must have felt during this incident. How will you get the wonder of this happening over to the children?
4. Pray for each child you teach, asking God to open their eyes to who Jesus is.
5. Choose appropriate visual aids.

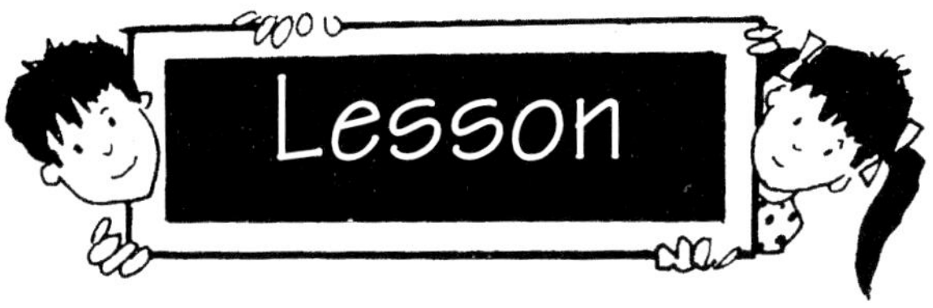

- Show children a bowl of water. Float something light on it, eg twig, then try a stone. Comment on the impossibility of a man being able to walk on water.

- Tell the story simply, showing pictures from a children's bible: "Here are Jesus' friends. They are in a boat. They are going accross the lake. It's night time. Where is Jesus? Look, he is coming to the boat. He's walking on the water. Could I do that? No. Only Jesus could walk on the water. Why? Because Jesus is God."

- **SAFETY:** Be sure to explain to the children that they cannot walk on water, and that they should not try to. Jesus can do it because he is God.

Prayer

Dear Lord Jesus, thank you for all the wonderful things you did when you lived on earth, Amen.

Visual aids

- bowl of water
- twig, stone.etc
- pictures from a Child's Story Bible

Activities

1. 1 sheet of paper per child with "Jesus is God" written along one long side. Child glues on blue waves, brown boat and a person – see page 20 for template.
2. Take a large container, eg cardboard box or plastic clothes basket. Put some children in the basket to pretend to be the disciples. Stand other children round in a circle to blow (the wind). Act out the story, stressing that Jesus was the only one who could walk on the water, because he was God.
3. Split children into 2 teams. Using 2 washing baskets with rope attached to either end, pull children to and fro across the "lake".

Reinforcement

1. Cut out as many different pictures of boats, ducks, fish, etc as you can find. Take a large sheet of paper and draw a blue line across the middle to represent the sea. Child glues boats, ducks, on top of water, fish in the water. Ask child, can you see any men? Why not? Comment on only having pictures of things that go on or in the sea. Men do not walk on the sea. Jesus walked on the lake. Why could Jesus do that? Jesus could walk on water because he is God.

2. Bathtime. Demonstrate things that float and things that sink. Ask child, can you walk on the water? No, you cannot walk on the water No one can walk on the water. Jesus walked on the water. Why could Jesus do that? Jesus could walk on the water because Jesus is God.

Jesus is God

Term 1 Lesson 10

Jesus made a sick man well

Lesson aim: to teach that Jesus could make a sick man well because Jesus is God

Teacher preparation

1. Read Matthew 8:1-4, Mark 1:40-44, Luke 5:12-16.
2. Answer the following questions:
   - how do you know the man had a recognised skin disease?
   - how did Jesus heal the man?
   - was this a miraculous healing?
3. Pray for each child you teach, asking God to open their eyes to who Jesus is.
4. Choose appropriate visual aids.

- Tell the story as follows, or in your own words: "Jesus met a sick man. All his skin hurt. Nobody wanted him. They didn't want to get sick like him. The man said:"Jesus, please make me better." Jesus touched him and said: "Get better". He was better right away. His skin didn't hurt any more. He was very happy. The doctors couldn't make him better. Jesus could. He didn't give him any medicine. He just said: "Get better." He could do that. Why? Because Jesus is God."

Prayer

Dear Lord Jesus, thank you for all the wonderful things you did when you lived on earth. Amen.

Visual aids

A paper bag puppet with a sad face on one side and a happy face on the other. Colour the sad face with blotches to show the skin disease.

Activities

1. Make a paper bag puppet for each child.
   - Draw a face on each side of the bag. Help child

   draw a sad mouth on one side and a happy mouth on the other side.
   - Ask child, how did the sick man feel?
   - Get child to turn hand so that sad face is visible. Tell child, Jesus made the sick man better. How did he feel when he was better?
   - Get child to show you happy face.

   "Jesus made the sick man well because Jesus is God".
2. Get children to sit on floor looking sad.
   - Say "Poor man, no one liked him because he was sick. Then Jesus said - get better!"
   - At "get better" all children jump up and dance around.
   - Do it as a game - see who can "get better " first.

Reinforcement

1. Use instances of family members/friends/animals being sick.
   - How did they get better? Comment on the cure taking time. Only Jesus could make people better instantly. Why could Jesus do this? Because Jesus is God.
2. Tell other stories about the miracles Jesus performed pointing out each time, only Jesus could do this, because Jesus is God.

Term 1 Lesson 11

Jesus made a lame man walk

Lesson aim: to teach that Jesus is God

Preparation

1. Read Matthew 9:1-7,
   Mark 2:1-12,
   Luke 5:17-26.
2. Answer the following questions:
   - whose faith did Jesus commend - the paralytic's or his friends'?
   - why did the teachers of the law accuse Jesus of blasphemy?
   - how did Jesus demonstrate his ability to forgive sins?
3. Think about the way in which this miracle demonstrates Jesus' divinity.
4. Pray for each child you teach, asking God to open their eyes to who Jesus is.
5. Choose appropriate visual aids.

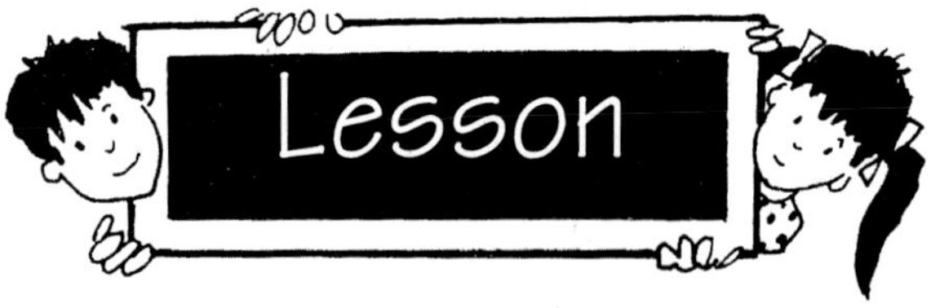

- Remind children that they have been learning about Jesus - that he could do things that no man could do - walk on water, heal the man with the bad skin. Jesus could do these things because he is God.

- Tell them the story as follows, or from your own words: " This man couldn't walk. He was ill. His legs didn't work. His friends wanted him to walk. They carried him to Jesus. They wanted Jesus to make him better. But Jesus was talking to lots of people. There was no room. They couldn't go into the house. So they made a hole in the roof. They carried the man through the hole. Jesus saw him. He said: "get up and go home". The man got up and went home. He could walk! Jesus made him better. Why? Because Jesus is God"

Prayer

Dear Lord Jesus, thank you for all the wonderful things you did when you lived on earth. Amen.

Visual aids

- Either pictures from a Child's Story Bible or models.
- A house can be made from a cardboard box with a flap cut in the top, or from children's building bricks/ Duplo/Lego. Use Playmobil or Fisher Price figures for the people.

Activities

1. Photocopy page 23 onto card for each child – or trace around man and transfer onto thin card. Cut out holes as indicated. Children put fingers through holes and walk man around.
   - Ask - who made the lame man walk?
   - who is Jesus? – Jesus is God.
2. Using models, get each child in turn to tell you the story. Younger children will need a lot of prompting! Finish off with same questions as No.1.

Reinforcement

1. Retell the story, using a member of the family as the paralysed man. Tie legs together so man cannot walk, crawl etc. Get other members of the family to help the "man" around. Point out to child how the 4 friends helped the man in the story.
2. Go over other stories of Jesus' miracles, pointing out each time that Jesus could do these things because he is God.

cut
out
cut
out

Term 1 Lesson 12

Jesus made a blind man see

Lesson aim: to teach that Jesus is God

Preparation

1. Read Mark 10:46-52.
2. Answer the following questions -
   ▪ how did Jesus know Bartimaeus was there?
   ▪ why did Bartimaeus not stop shouting out when the people rebuked him?
   ▪ was Bartimaeus clear about what he wanted Jesus to do for him?
   ▪ how did Jesus heal Bartimaeus?
3. Think about the power of Jesus' word to heal Bartimaeus. Reflect on the power of God's word to transform lives.
4. Pray for each child you teach, asking God to help you teach his word clearly.
5. Choose appropriate visual aids.

- Remind children that they have been hearing about the wonderful things Jesus could do - walk on water, make the man with the bad skin better, make the lame man walk. Jesus could do all these things because Jesus is God.

- "Jesus was going along the road. Lots of people were with him. There was a man by the road. He was sitting down. What is wrong with him? Look at his eyes: he can't see. The man heard Jesus. He shouted: "Jesus, help me!" The people said: "Be quiet," but the man shouted louder. Jesus heard him. He said: "What do you want?" The man said: "Please make me see." And the man could see (alter eyes on picture). Only Jesus could make him better. Why? Because Jesus is God.

Prayer

Thank you, Lord Jesus that you could make the blind man see. Amen.

Visual aids

- Picture of blind man (page 25)
  ▪ Cut off eye strip. Cut off tab section, fold inhalf and glue over hatched area of eye strip.
  ▪ Cut out eye sockets and cut along 4 dotted lines.
  ▪ Insert eye strip so that irises can be pulled across to make man see.

Activities

1. Play I-spy. "Who can see something green?" etc. Anything that is the stated colour is a correct answer .Comment on the man in the story not being able to see. Who made him see? Why could Jesus make him see?
2. Get children to sit on floor with eyes closed. As soon as teacher says - Jesus made the blind man see - children jump up. Ask - who made the blind man see? Why could Jesus make the blind man see?

Reinforcement

1. Blindfold an adult or older child. Get young child to bring various items for blind-folded person to touch and identify. Talk about being blind. Ask - who made the blind man see? Why could Jesus make the blind man see?
2. Go over the stories of Jesus' miracles using a Child's Story Bible. Comment each time that Jesus could do this because Jesus is God.

Jesus made a blind man see
because Jesus is God

Mark 10:46-52

Term 1 Lesson 13

Jesus made a deaf man hear

Lesson aim: to teach that Jesus is God

Teacher Preparation

1. Read Mark 7:31-37.
2. Answer the following questions:-
   - who had faith in this story?
   - why did Jesus take the man away from the crowd?
   - how did Jesus heal the man?
3. Reflect on Jesus' power to heal, remembering that he did not heal every deaf man. What was the point of the miracles? (see John 20:30-31).
4. Pray for each child you teach, asking God to open their eyes to who Jesus is.
5. Choose appropriate visual aids.

- Remind children that they have been hearing about the wonderful things Jesus did - walked on water, made a sick man well, a lame man walk, a blind man see. After each one say, "Could you do that?" "Jesus could do that" "Why could Jesus do that?"etc.

- One day some people brought a sick man to see Jesus. This man was deaf - he could not hear and he couldn't speak. They said to Jesus: "Please make the deaf man hear." Jesus took the man away from the crowd. He touched him and said, "Open up". At once the man could hear and speak well. Jesus could do this because Jesus is God.

Prayer

Thank you, Jesus, that you could make this sick man better because you are God. Amen.

Visual Aids

- Picture of a man with a sad face (page 27).
  - Cut out mouth and secure to picture with a split pin so that mouth is sad. Once man is healed, turn mouth to happy.

Activities

1. Make a squeaker. Each child requires a yoghurt pot; a length of string; a piece of wrapping paper; glue.
   - Prior to lesson cut rectangles of paper the size required to go round the yoghurt pot. Pierce a hole in the centre of the base of each yoghurt pot.
   - Children glue wrapping paper round yoghurt pot
   - Push a piece of string through the hole in the pot and tie a knot at both ends.
   - Draw the string through the hole to produce a squeaking sound.(Pot needs to be held over the ear). Younger children may need help with pulling the string

- Show the children one made prior to the lesson.
- Point out to the children that the deaf man could not hear anything until Jesus healed him. Ask "Why could Jesus make the deaf man hear?"

2. Have a tape of music and various sounds. Comment on the deaf man being unable to hear anything. Ask - Who made the deaf man hear? Why could Jesus make the deaf man hear?

Reinforcement

1. Go for a walk and identify the various sounds. The deaf man could not hear that. Who made the deaf man hear? Why could Jesus make the deaf man hear?
2. Cover child's ears with your hands and whisper to them. Take hands away. Ask child if they heard what you said. Ask - would you like to be like that? The deaf man was like that. Who made the deaf man hear?
3. Read stories about Jesus' miracles from a Child's Story Bible. Ask each time, Why could Jesus do this? Because Jesus is God.

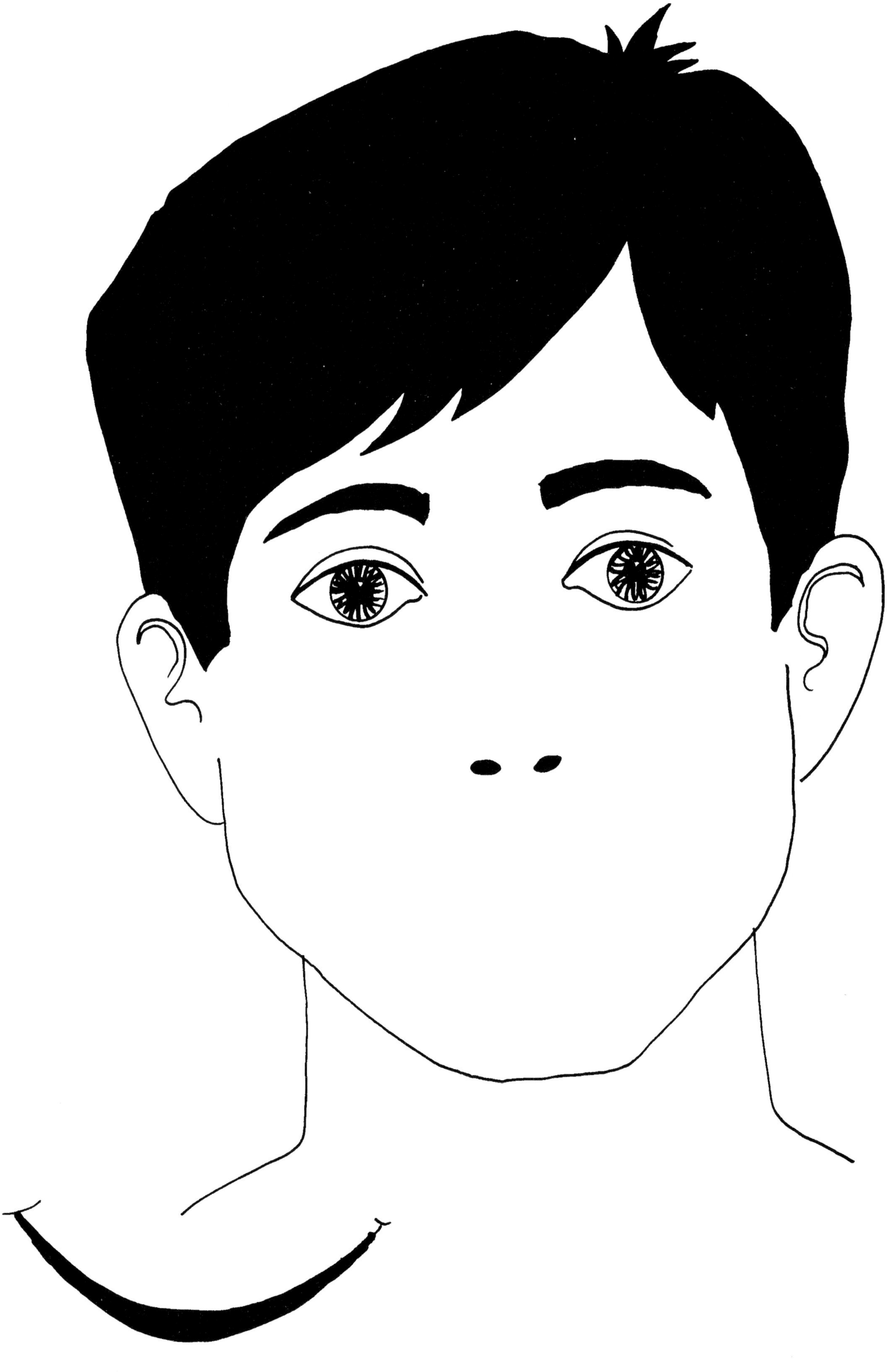

Term 1 Lesson 14

God looks after me while I play

Lesson Aim: to know that God is interested in everything I do and looks after me

Preparation

1. Read Psalm 16:1-11, Psalm 5:11-12, Psalm 11:4
2. Answer the following questions:
   - what do you learn about God from Psalm 16?
   - does God give his people good things?
   - what does Psalm 5 v11-12 teach about God's protection?
   - is God aware of what is happening in his world? (Psalm 11v4)
3. Meditate on the picture of God gained from the above Scriptures.
4. Pray for each child you teach, that they will learn that God is always with them.
5. Choose appropriate visual aids.

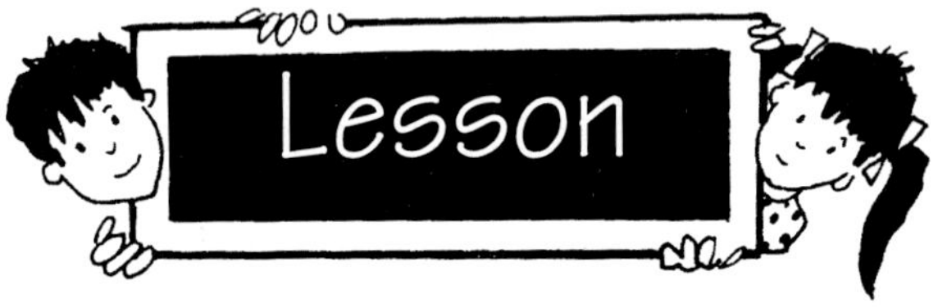

- Ask children about playing – who likes to play with their toys?
- what toy do you like best?
- who gives you your toys?
- Look at some different toys
- Show pictures of children playing in the park. at home,etc.
- Point out to children that God knows all they do and looks after them while they play.

Prayer

Thank, you, God, that we can have fun with our toys. Amen

Visual Aids

- toys
- pictures of children playing

Activities

1. Give each child a sheet of coloured paper with "God looks after me while I play" written along the bottom. Cut out pictures of toys from magazines/catalogues. Children choose pictures and glue them onto their sheet.
2. While children are playing, remind them that God knows what they are doing and is looking after them.

Reinforcement

1. Give your child a piggy-back. Tell them they are a monkey up a tree. Have someone else be a bear/lion and try and catch the monkey, while you protect him/her. (Be careful not to frighten a sensitive child). Ask - who looks after us?
2. Use times when you play with your child to reinforce the fact that God knows what they are doing and is looking after them.

God looks after me while I sleep

Lesson Aim: to teach that God is always with me and looks after me while I sleep

Preparation

1. Read Psalm 121:1-8, Psalm 4:8, Psalm 139:8-12
2. Answer the following questions:
   - what do you learn about God from Psalm 121?
   - how does Psalm 4 v8 help a child who is afraid of the dark?
   - is there anywhere I can go and God is not there?
3. Many children are afraid of the dark. Think about the way you can reassure the children you teach.
4. Pray for each child you teach, that they will learn that God is always with them.
5. Choose appropriate visual aids.

- Talk about bedtime.
- Who likes going to bed? Why? etc.
- Point out the need to go to sleep when we are tired.
- Get children to lie down and pretend to go to sleep.
- Do you have a story when you go to bed?
- Open book and talk to children about the importance of thanking God for the day before we go to sleep.
- Point out that - God made the dark so that we can sleep. God doesn't sleep, so can look after us when we sleep

Prayer

Thank you, God, for looking after me when I sleep.

Visual Aid

Child's Story Bible.

Activities

1. Make cardboard beds - (backs of cereal packets are the right thickness). Cut along solid lines, fold along dotted lines.Glue at corners (or staple)
   - Prior to lesson make 1 pipecleaner figure for each child. Child can then put figure into bed and cover with a strip of material.

2. Put dollies and teddies to bed and sing a lullaby to them. Read a story. Reinforce the message: "who looks after us while we sleep? God does."

Reinforcement

1. Count number of beds in house.Go round with child asking each time - who sleeps in this bed? God knows that. God looks after............ while he/she is asleep.
2. Use bed time to reinforce - who looks after you while you sleep? God does. There is no need to be frightened of the dark. God never sleeps, so God can look after you while you sleep.

Term 1 Lesson 16

God looks after me while I travel

Lesson Aim: to teach that God looks after me everywhere I go

Preparation

1. Read Psalm 139:1-12, Genesis 28:10-15, Romans 8:31-38, Hebrews 13:5-8.
2. Answer the following questions:
   - From Psalm 139 list all the places where God knows what is happening to you.
   - write down God's promise to Jacob in Genesis 28
   - in Romans 8 what does Paul cite as the basis of our confidence that God will never leave us? List the things that are unable to separate us from the love of God.
   - Hebrews 13:5 quotes God's promise to Joshua (Joshua 1:5).
   - why can we trust this promise today?
3. Think about God's promise in Hebrews 13:5. What difference should this make to your life?
4. Pray for each child you teach, thanking God that he loves them and cares for them.
5. Choose appropriate visual aids.

Visual Aids

Pictures of different types of transport.

Activities

1. Make a bus from 2 rows of chairs. Sit children in rows and pretend to be bus driver, etc.Make a line of children into a train. Chug round the room, stopping at stations.
   - Each time ask - Does God know where you are when you are in the ....?
2. A transport mobile - make for children to take home.
   - Each child requires a wire coat hanger and sheets 31 and 32 photocopied onto card.
   - Cut out transport shapes and attach each one to a length of thread.
   - Children colour/decorate shapes, which are then attached to the coat hanger. **NB**. The threads need to be different lengths so that shapes hang at different levels.
3. Sing "the wheels on the bus go round and round."

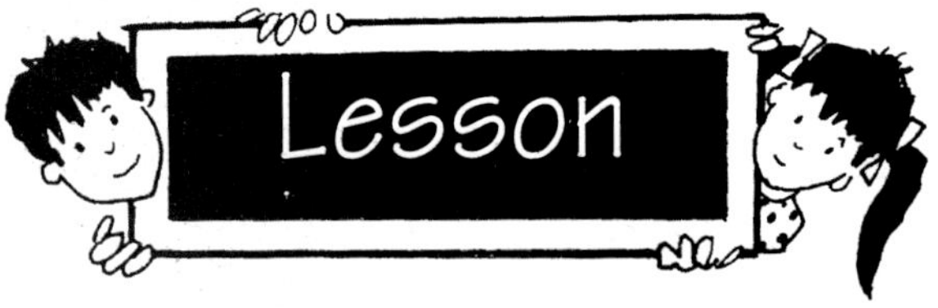

- Show children pictures of different types of transport - car, bus, train, boat, plane.
- Ask children to identify each one.
- Talk about who has been in each one.
- Talk about journeys - do they like going on journeys? Where have they been, etc.
- Talk about God being everywhere, so God can look after them wherever they go.
- Ask them - was God there when you came to church (or wherever) today?
- God knew you were in the car / on the bus / walking along the road, etc.

Prayer

Thank you, God, for looking after me everywhere I go.

Reinforcement

1. At start of journeys remind child that God looks after us wherever we are. Thank God in a simple prayer.
2. Cut out pictures of different modes of transport. Child glues them onto a large sheet of paper. Go through the pictures - does God look after me when I am on...?
3. Go on a pretend journey with your child. This can be done moving around the house. Reinforce the fact of God looking after us wherever we are. (The journey can be made more exciting by using soft toys to be animals in a safari park, etc)

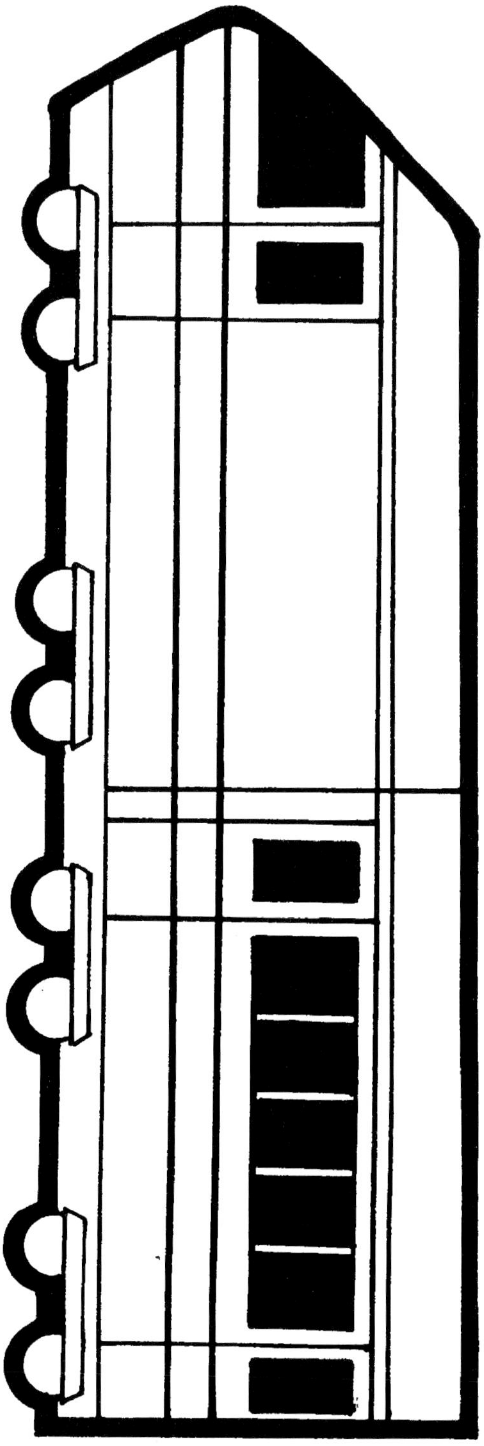

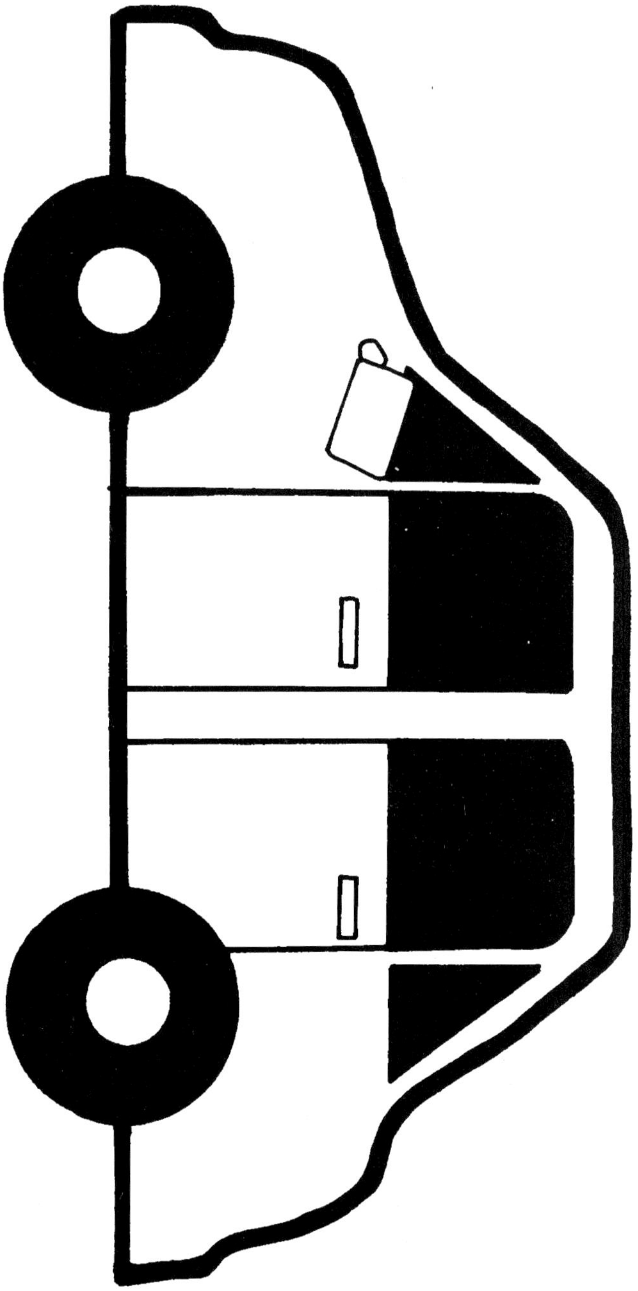

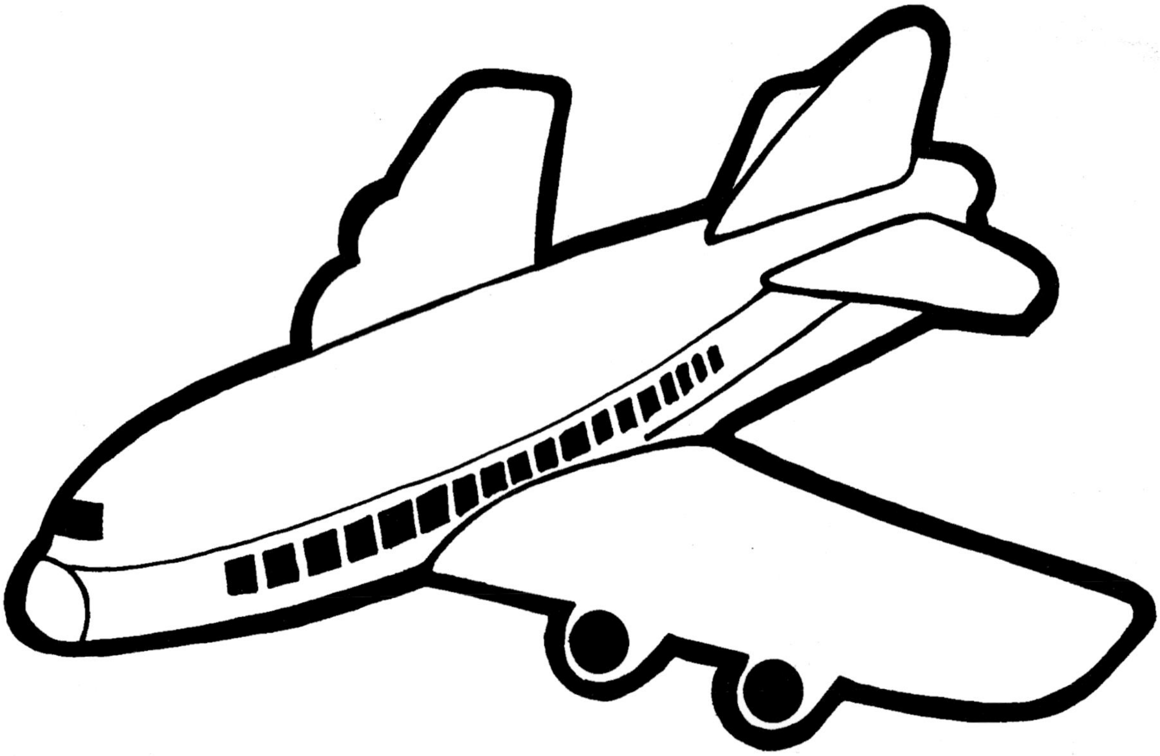

Term 1 Lesson 17

God gives me food and drink

Lesson aim: to teach that God provides for my daily needs

Preparation

1. Read Matthew 6:25-34
2. Answer the following questions:
   - why are we not to worry about what we will eat or drink?
   - does this mean we should not plan in advance?
   - what does "worry" mean?
   - what should be our first priority?
3. Think about the children you teach and the confidence they display in their parents - do they ever worry about where their next meal is coming from? Do you have this same confidence that God will supply your needs?
4. Pray for the children you teach, thanking God for their example in this situation.
5. Choose appropriate visual aids.

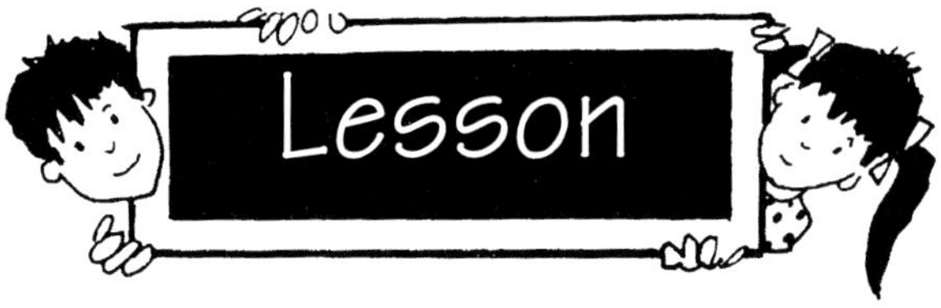

- Have some pictures of food growing.
- Talk to children about God causing the food to grow.
- Show pictures of different types of food - in tins, packets, fresh.
- Ask - who gives us our food? If the answer is "Mummy" - comment that Mummy is only able to give us our food because God made the food grow in the first place.
- Do the same with a picture of a reservoir and a glass of water.
- Talk about the need to thank God for our food.
- End with biscuits and a drink, thanking God for the food before consuming it.

Prayer

Dear God, thank you for our food, Amen.

Visual Aids

- pictures of food growing
- pictures of different types of food (packets, tins, fresh)
- pictures of rivers, reservoirs
- glass of water
- biscuits and drinks

Activities

1. Have a doll's tea party.
2. Give each child a sheet of paper with "thank you, God, for my food" written along the bottom..
   - Cut out pictures of food and drinks from magazines. Allow children to choose pictures and glue them onto the sheet.
   - Reinforce — who gives us our food? God gives us our food.

Reinforcement

1. Say thank you to God for your food before every meal (if you don't already do this).
2. When preparing food, allow child to see what you are doing (and help if appropriate). Ask - who gives us our food?
3. When shopping, ask child "Who makes the food grow?"

Term 2 Lesson 1

God made the sky

Lesson Aim: to know that God made the sky

Preparation

1. Read Psalm 8, Psalm 19:1-6
2. Answer the following questions:
   - what does Psalm 8 teach about God?
   - what does Psalm 8 teach about man?
   - from Psalm 19:1-6, how does the sky reveal God's glory?
3. Think about the wonderful world God has made and the importance of teaching this to the children.
4. Pray for each child you teach, that God will open his/her eyes to the glory of his creation.
5. Choose appropriate visual aids.

- Show children a big picture of the sky.
- Talk to children about the sky and get each child to point to it in turn.
- What colour is the sky? Is it always blue? Why is it different colours? What do you see in the sky? Clouds, Sun, Birds, Rainbow, Stars, Moon, Rain (Aeroplanes!) Thunder, Lightning, Wind, Snow, Hailstones. Stick on pictures of each item as you talk about it. (If possible, have different background pictures - a fine day, night sky, thundery sky).
- Get children to come and point to different things.
- Talk about God making each thing.

Prayer

Thank you, God, for making the sky and everything in it. Amen.

Visual aids

Pictures

Activities

1. Give each child a piece of paper with "God made the sky" written on it. Give each child an envelope containing cut outs of moon, sun, stars, to glue onto picture. Cotton wool balls can be glued on as clouds.
2. Make a rainbow, using paints and thick brushes.
3. Have pictures of various items - some you would see in the sky, eg clouds, moon, birds, plane, helicopter, and some you would not, eg bus, car, flower, house. Have 2 boards - 1 with a big sheet of blue paper for the sky and 1 without. Hold up the pictures of the various items one at a time, asking - does this go in the sky? Get children to say what item is as well as whether or not it should be in the sky. Ask, who made the sky? Pin item onto appropriate board.

Reinforcement

1. Go for a walk and look at the sky. What can you see? Who made the sky? Repeat the process at night, looking out of a window.
2. Look at pictures of the sky in children's story books. Ask, "Who made the sky?"
3. Make a collage of the sky, using cut outs from magazines. Ask "Who made the sky?"

Term 2 Lesson2

God made the sea

Lesson Aim: to teach that God made the sea

Preparation

1. Read Genesis 1:1 -2 v4.
2. Answer the following questions:-
   - how did God create the various parts (vv3,6,9)?
   - what did God think of his creation (vv 4,10)?
3. Think about the power of God's word and the wonder of his creation.
4. Pray for each child you teach, asking God to open his/her eyes to the glories of his creation.
5. Choose appropriate visual aids.

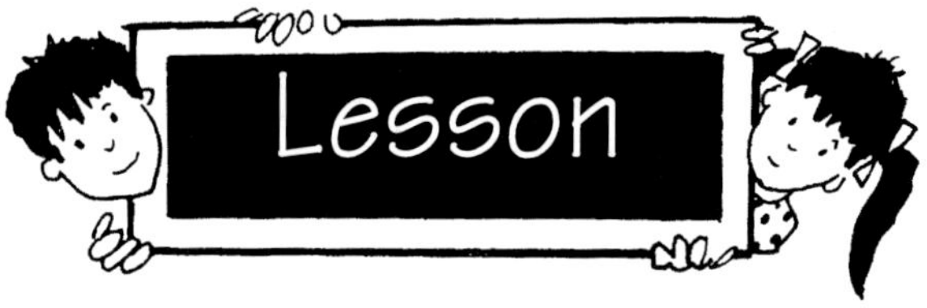

- Show children a big picture of the sea.
- Talk to the children about the sea and get each child to point to it.
- Ask "Who made the sea?
- What do we find in the sea? - fish, seaweed, shells.
- Glue pictures of the various items on to the background as you talk about them. For each picture ask, "Who made the sea?"
- Get children to come out and point to various items. Show children seashells. Talk about all the different things God made.

Prayer

Thank you, God, for making the sea and everything in it. Amen.

Visual Aids

Big background of sea and pictures of items found in the sea.

Activities

1. Give each child a sheet of blue paper with "God made the sea" written on it. Have an envelope of cut outs of fish, weed, etc from magazines for children to glue onto the paper.
2. Repeat activity 3 from "God made the sky", using sea instead of sky.
3. Ask children, how do you travel on the sea? Make a boat by surrounding an area big enough to hold all the children with cushions /chairs /tables. Remind children of who looks after them when they travel. Pretend that big waves are coming, etc.

Reinforcement

1. Make a collage of the sea using pictures cut from magazines. Ask - who made the sea?etc.
2. Bathtime. Demonstrate action of the sea using toy boats and making waves, etc. Ask - who made to sea? Refer back to Jesus walking on the water – why could Jesus do that?
3. Look at pictures of the sea and things that you find in the sea. Ask - who made the sea?

Term 2 Lesson 3

God made the earth

Lesson Aim: to teach that God made the earth

Preparation

1. Read Genesis 1:1- 2:4.
2. Answer the following questions:
   - how did God make the earth and plants (vv 9,11)?
   - what did God think of the earth (vv10,12)?
3. Think about the power of God's word and the wonderful earth he has made. Think about the diversity of plants.
4. Pray for each child you teach, asking God to help you demonstrate the wonders of his creation.
5. Choose appropriate visual aids.

- Show children a big background of earth and sky. Talk to children about what they can see - the grass - and get children to point to it in turn. Ask if they have grass at home. Tell them God made the grass.
- Add mountains and rocks to picture - ask, who made ......? What do we find growing in the ground? trees, bushes, flowers, etc. Stick on each item as you talk about it, asking, who made ....? Get children to point to different items.Real flowers and leaves can be used. Talk about God making each thing.

Prayer

Thank you, God, for making the earth and all that grows in it. Amen.

Visual Aids

Pictures
Flowers and leaves.

Activities

1. Get children to pretend to be flowers growing. (This is best done to music). They start by curling up on the floor as the seed, then gradually uncurl, stretching up to the light and opening arms as leaves. Ask, who made the flowers?
2. Give each child a sheet of paper with "God made the earth" written on it. Child glues cut outs of flowers, trees, etc onto paper. Reinforce - God made that.
3. Place a series of mats from one end of the room to the other. The mats are the land and the floor is the sea. Ask who made the sea? Who made the land? Children have to get from one end of the room to the other without falling in the sea.

Reinforcement

1. Place a plastic container of soil on a newspaper on the table. Empty some of the soil onto the newspaper. Feel it in your fingers and move it around. What do you find? Encourage child to do the same "Who made ....?"
   - What grows in soil? - show seeds and bulbs.

   Use the soil to make a hill, then a mountain. "Who made the hills?"etc.
   - Finish by planting seeds/bulbs and watching them grow over a period of time.
2. Go for a walk and point out all the things God made.
3. When looking at picture books, remind child, "Who made that?"

Term 2 Lesson 4

God made the animals

Lesson Aim: to teach that God made all living creatures

Preparation

1. Read Genesis 1:1 - 2:4.
2. Answer the following questions:-
   - how did God make the creatures (vv 20,24)
   - what did God think of his creation (vv 21,25)?
3. Think about the way God created this world and the diversity of his creation.
4. Pray for each child you teach asking God to open his/her eyes to the wonders of his creation.
5. Choose appropriate visual aids.

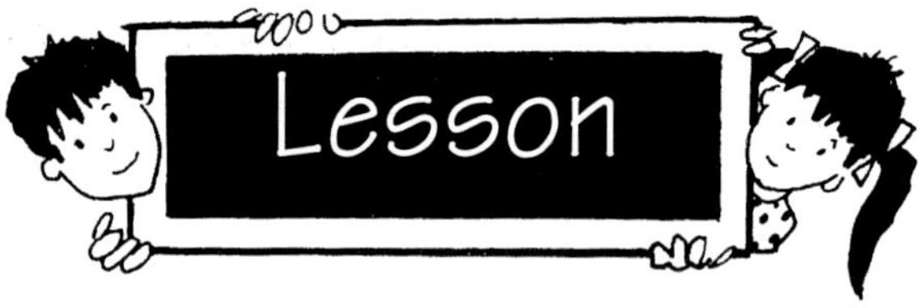

- Show children pictures of different animals. Ask child to say which animal it is. Then ask, who made the ....? Use the background pictures of land, sky and sea and place fish in the sea, birds in the air, animals on the land. Each time ask, "Who made the ....?"

Prayer

Thank you, God, for making the animals. Amen.

Visual Aids

- Pictures
- You may have a pet you could bring in to show the children.

Activities

1. Finger rhyme based on "Two little dickybirds":

Two little dicky birds not knowing what to do
(hold up both index fingers)
One asked the other, who made you?
(bend top of index finger in time with who made you)
One little dicky bird flew into a tree
(put second index finger on top of your head)
I know the answer, God made me.
(bend top of 2nd index finger in time with God made me)

2. Get children to pretend to be different animals, eg Who can be a sheep? (Children go on all fours saying Baa,baa). Who made the sheep? Who can be a fish? (Children squirm on the floor like a fish) Who made the fish?
3. Play, Old MacDonald had a farm.
4. Make an animal mobile for child to take home (most of this needs to be made in advance).
   - Photocopy pages 39 and 40 onto different coloured card – 1 set for each child. Cut out animals and put each onto a piece of cotton. Child can colour or glue gummed shapes/pieces of material onto animals. Attach animals one under the other in a line to make the mobile.

Reinforcement

1. Look at all the animals in child's bedroom. Are they real or toys? Look at all the animals /birds/insects you can see outside. Are they real or toys? Who made the animals?
2. Look at picture books and name as many different animals as possible. Who made the animals?
3. Pretend to be different animals and ask child to guess which animal you are - actions as well as sounds. Ask - Who made the......?

God made the Animals

Term 2 Lesson 5

God made me

Lesson aim: to know that God made me

Preparation

1. Read Genesis 1:1 - 2:4.
2. Answer the following questions:-
   - how did God make man (v26)
   - what does it mean, to be in the image of God?
   - what job did God give man?
3. Think about what it means to be made in the image of God, and able to have a relationship with him.
4. Pray for each child you teach, that they will learn more about the God who made them.
5. Choose appropriate visual aids.

- Show children a big background of land and sky. Remind children that God made it. Add trees, plants, etc reminding children that God made them. Add birds and animals, reminding children that God made them. Add a man, a woman, a boy, a girl, a baby - God made them and God made me.

Prayer

Thank you, God, for making me, Amen.

Visual aids

Pictures

Activities

1. Make a headband for each child. Cut a sheet of A4 coloured card in half. Write "God made me" on one half. Children can decorate with gummed paper shapes and glitter pens. Staple or glue 2 halves together to make a headband (worn like a crown)

2. Teach the following rhyme:

God made the sky
(point upwards)
God made the sea
(ripple fingers)
God made the animals
(down on all fours)
And God made me.
(jump up and bang chest with fist)

Reinforcement

1. Show child pictures of him/her at different ages. Who is this? Who made .....? Make a big picture from the photos with child's name followed by "God made me" in the middle.
2. Ask child to draw a self-portrait. Add a hand print. Write child's name followed by "God made me".

Term 2 Lesson 6

God knows my name and what I look like

Lesson aim: to show the children that God knows them individually and intimately

Preparation

1. Read Psalm 139:1-18.
2. Answer the following questions:
   - what does God know about me?
   - at what stage in my life did God first know me?
   - is there anything that God doesn't know about me?
3. Think about the wonder of God knowing me from the moment of conception.
4. Pray for each child you teach, that they will come to know the God who made them.
5. Choose appropriate visual aids.

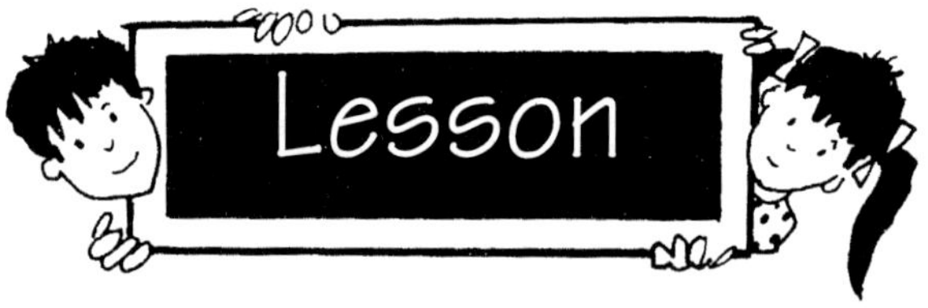

- Sit the children down in small groups, each with an adult. Ask each child the following questions:-
  - What is your name?
  - Have you got a brother or sister?
  - Do you have a favourite toy?
  - What do you like to eat?
  - Do you go to playschool?
  - What colour is your hair?
  - What colour are your eyes? etc
- Following each answer ,say "God knows that".
- Point out that God made us, loves us and knows all about us.

Prayer

Thank you, God, that you know all about me and you still love me. Amen.

Activities

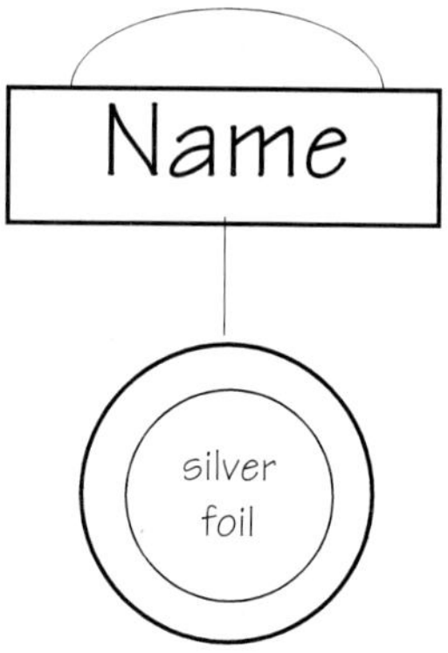

1. Make a mobile in 2 parts - join them together with thread. Child's name is written on the rectangle and child decorates it with coloured stars. Put a circle of silver foil in middle of bottom section to act as a mirror.Write "God knows what I look like" round outside.
2. Play true/false. Children make a circle. Call out child's name. Child comes into middle of circle.Say N. has green hair (or black, or orange etc.) ! Is that true? Children call out yes/no. Reinforce with correct colour then say God knows that. Use clothing, etc and do something for each child.

Reinforcement

1. Write child's name in large letters at top of piece of paper. Child helps colour/decorate name. Underneath draw a face - a circle with 2 eyes, nose and mouth.Colour eyes the same colour as child's eyes, Add hair of appropriate style and colour.Refer back to lessons on who made my eyes, etc.
2. Using paint make palm/hand prints on a piece of paper. Compare yours with the child's. Point out each one is different. God made us that way and God knows all about us.
3. Write the name of each member of the family on separate pieces of paper and place in a container. Ask child to take one out. Read the name on the paper. Ask, "Whose name is that?" "God knows that". Repeat till all names have been drawn out.
4. Look at a selection of family photos. Ask child to identify him/herself. Reinforce - God knows your name and what you look like.
5. Look in a mirror with your child. Ask them questions about themselves, saying "God knows that "each time.

Term 2 Lesson 7

God knows I am growing

Lesson aim: to teach that God knows all about me — about all the changes in my appearance as I grow

Preparation

1. Read Psalm 139:1-18.
2. Answer the following questions:
- what does God know about me?
- what did God know about me before I was born?
- does God know what is happening to me now?
3. Think about what it means to have a God who knows everything about me, yet loves me enough to die for me.
4. Pray for each child you teach, that God will enable you to teach clearly and lovingly.
5. Choose appropriate visual aids.

Activities

1. Have a selection of different clothes and shoes, adults, big children, babies. Ask children to dress up in different clothes - why don't they fit?
2. Make a "growing" child.
   Photocopy pages 44 and 45 onto card for each child. Cut out body, appropriate legs, head and arms. Fold body strip like a fan and attach between head, arms and legs. Draw on appropriate hair and colour figure. Hold onto head and pull gently on legs to watch child grow.

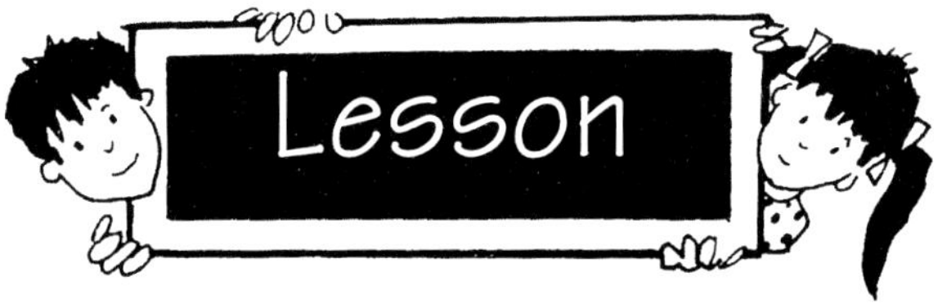

- Talk to the children about what they were like as babies - size, no teeth, little hair, what they ate, etc. Show pictures of babies. Talk about how they have changed - physically, ability to talk, ability to feed themselves,etc. Have pictures of toddlers/children at different stages.
- Show pictures of later stages - adolescence, adulthood, school children,etc. Conclude by pointing out that it is God who decides what we will look like as we grow older - colour of hair, height, etc. You can use a height chart to see how tall they all are, but some children may not want to do this.

Prayer

Thank you, God, that you know all about me. Amen.

Visual aids

- Pictures of people at varying stages of development - babies to adults.
- Height chart (optional).

Reinforcement

1. Look through child's baby book or old family photos. Point out how child has grown. God knows that.
2. Try on child's old clothes. "Look how much you have grown!" "God knows that".

Body Strip - cut out and fold in concertina

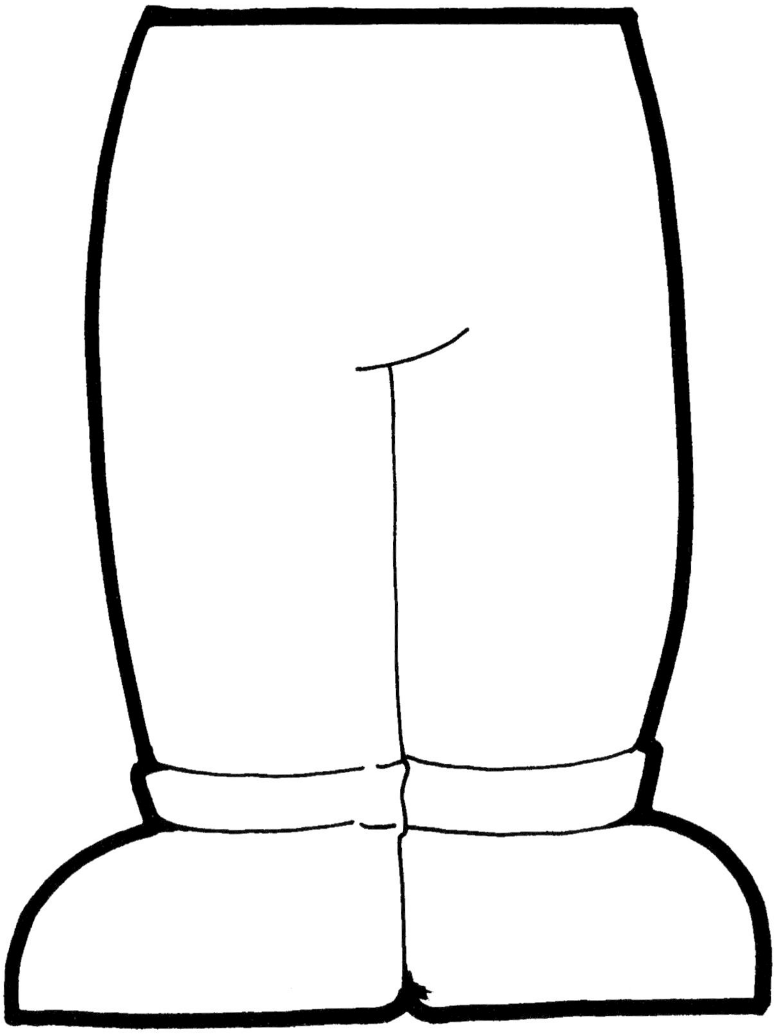

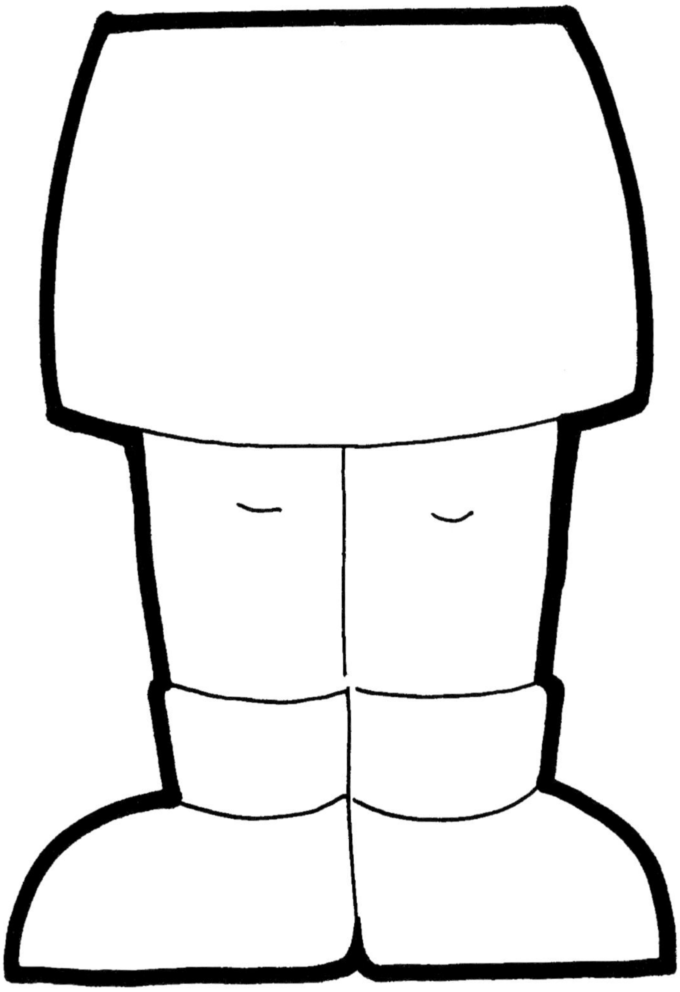

God knows where I live

Lesson aim: to show the children that God knows all about them

Preparation

1. Read Psalm 139:1-18.
2. Answer the following questions:-
   - what does God know about me?
   - where is God?
3. Think about God's omnipresence. How can you make this real to a small child?
4. Pray for each child you teach, that they will learn that God is always with them.
5. Choose appropriate visual aids.

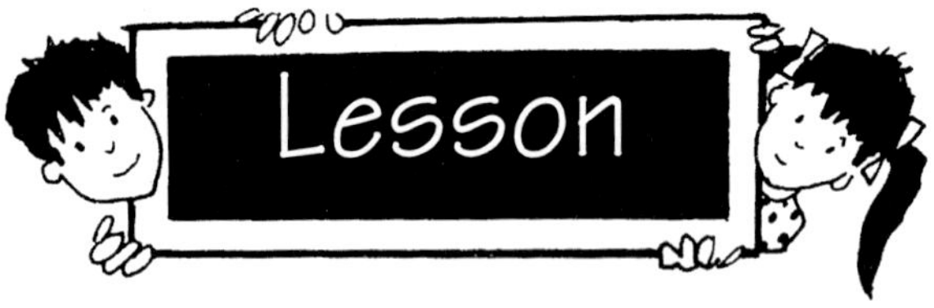

- Show children pictures of different types of housing - flats, terraced houses, semis, detached houses, etc.Talk about the types of houses the children live in, whether or not there is a garden, etc.
- Talk about how lucky they are to have somewhere to live, a nice warm bed to sleep in, etc. Point out that God knows where they live.

Prayer

Thank you, God, that you know all about me. Amen.

Visual aids

Pictures of different types of housing.

Activities

1. Cut out pictures of houses, flats, etc from magazines. Give each child a circle of coloured card with "God knows where I live" written on it. Punch a hole at the top and hang circle from a length of wool long enough to go round child's neck. Child chooses a picture of the type of house he/she lives in and glues it onto the plain side of the circle. Child wears it like a pendant.
2. Build houses from Lego/Duplo building blocks.
3. Make a house from an old shoe box. The lid is the roof. Cut a door that will open and close and holes for windows. Glue a piece of paper onto lid with "God knows where I live" written on it. (Shoe boxes are available from your local shoe shop on request).

Reinforcement

1. Ask child "Who lives next door?" "Who lives over the road?" etc."God knows that".
2. Show child pictures of different living quarters;
   - bird's nest
   - dog's kennel
   - beaver's dam
   - horse's stable
   - cow barn
   - pig stye
   - hen house

   Match the animal with the house. God knows where the hen lives, etc. God knows where you live.

God knows when I am naughty

Lesson aim: to teach the children that
God knows all about us, even when we are naughty
God forgives us if we are truly sorry
God loves us, even when we are naughty

Preparation

1. Read Psalm 139:1-4, 1John 1:8 - 2:2, Romans 8:38 -39.
2. Answer the following questions:
   - we sin in thought, action and word. Are any of these areas hidden from God?
   - 1John 1:9 details God's promise. What is it? What is required from me?
   - how can my sins be forgiven? (1John 2:1-2)
   - does my sinning stop God loving me? (Romans 8:38-39).
3. Think about the price that Jesus paid on your behalf.
4. Pray for each child in your care, asking God for wisdom to enable you to teach this important lesson.
5. Choose appropriate visual aids.

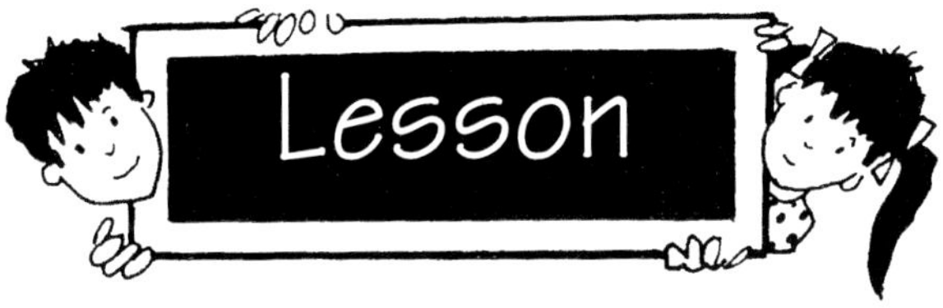

- Show children pictures of children being deliberately naughty (not just careless). Point out that their behaviour is naughty.
- Use finger puppets to act out a naughty scene (see visual aids).
- Is Mummy happy when I am naughty? No
- Is Daddy happy when I am naughty? No
- Is God happy when I am naughty? No
- Even though we can't see God, he knows everything we do. God knows when we are naughty. The naughty things we do do not please God, they make him very sad.
- When we do naughty things we have to say sorry to daddy/ mummy/ friends (give examples) . And we have to say sorry to God.
- If I say sorry to God he forgives me. That means that he will make things right again and forget that I did that naughty thing. But I must be really sorry and try not to do that naughty thing again.
- God helps me to be good, and even when I am naughty God still loves me.

Prayer

Dear God, thank you for loving me, even when I am naughty. Amen.

Visual aids

- Pictures of children doing naughty things -
  - e.g. snatching toys
  - hitting / fighting
  - taking what isn't theirs

Finger Puppets - make from a piece of paper, folded in half and cut out to fit on a finger. Sellotape or staple sides together. Draw on face.

Activities

1. Learn action rhyme:

God loves me when I'm happy
(big smile)
God loves me when I'm sad
(sad face)
God loves me when I'm very good
(clap hands or nod for being good)
and even when I'm bad
(wag finger or shake head for being bad)

2. Make a big pendant.
   Cut out a big heart shape from red card. Punch a hole in the top and thread with a piece of wool long enough to go round child's neck. On one side of heart write "God loves me". Give child a picture of a naughty child to glue on back and write "even when I am naughty".

Reinforcement

1. Use times when child is naughty to point out that mummy and daddy are sad, so is God. Go over the need to say sorry and give child a hug straight after punishment. Reinforce - you love your child, even when he/she is naughty, and so does God.
2. Praise good behaviour.

Term 2 Lesson 10

How does God speak to me?

Lesson aim: to teach that we learn about God from the Bible, which is his word

Preparation

1. Read 2 Timothy 3:14-17, 2 Peter 1:19-21, Psalm 119:89-112
2. Answer the following questions:
   - at what age does Paul consider you should start learning from the Bible?
   - where does Paul say the Bible is from?
   - what does Paul say the Bible does for us?
   - why does Peter say we should pay attention to the Bible?
   - from Psalm 119:89-112 list the things you discover about the Bible.
3. Think about the way you use the Bible. Do you spend time reading it?
4. Pray for each child you teach, that God will help you to teach his word accurately.
5. Choose appropriate visual aids.

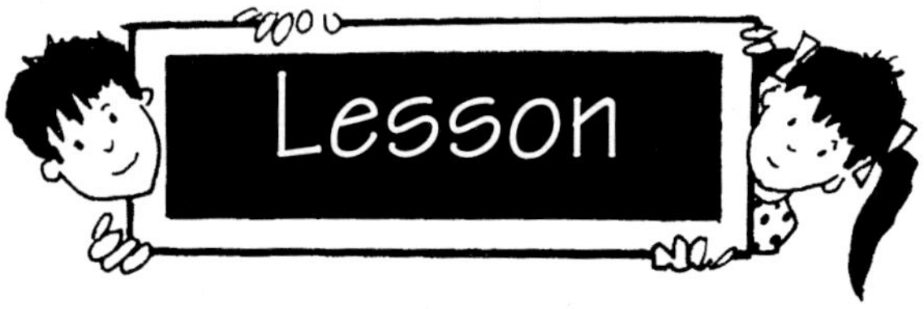

- We have been learning lots of things about God.
- How do we know what God is like?
- God has told us all about himself in a special book, called the Bible (show children a Bible).
- This book tells us all about God.
- It tells us God made everything (recap on what God has made).
- The Bible tells me that God knows all about me
  - he knows my name and what I look like
  - he knows where I live
  - God knows when I am good
  - God knows when I am naughty.
- The Bible tells me that God loves me, even more than mummy and daddy love me. The Bible tells me that God looks after me all the time - even when I am asleep.

Prayer

Thank you, God, for the Bible. Amen.

Visual aids

Pictures of the different things that the Bible tells me about.

Activities

1. Make a simple Bible: Give each child a coloured sheet of A4 paper folded in half. Accross the inside write 'God' in big letters. Each child needs a piece of white paper. On which is written "The Bible". Child glues the Bible on front of folded sheet of paper and colours or decorates the name God inside. Ask: "What does the Bible tell me about?" Open the 'Bible' and say "God!"
2. Have several books, some of them of Bible stories, some not. Hold up the book and tell children what it is about. "Is this a book about God?" "Is this a Bible book?"

Reinforcement

1. At bedtime, read child a Bible story. Point out that this is the way God speaks to us.

Term 2 Lesson 11

How do I speak to God?

Lesson aim: to introduce the children to the idea of talking to God

Preparation

1. Read Luke 11:1-13.
2. Answer the following questions:-
   - why do we need to be taught how to pray?
   - in Luke 11:2-4, whose concerns come first?
   - why does the man get up and give his friend bread?
   - what sort of gifts do human fathers give their children?
   - why do these 2 parables encourage us to pray?
3. Think about the way you pray. Are your prayers God-centred or self-centred?
4. Pray for each child you teach, that God will help you teach them to pray.
5. Choose appropriate visual aids.

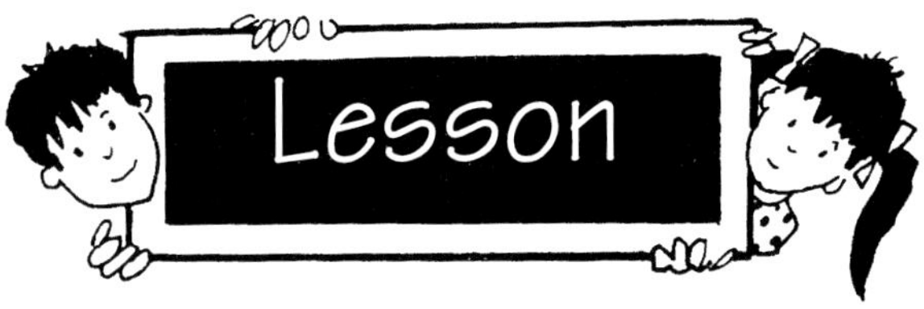

- God loves us so much that he wants to talk to us. That is why he gave us the Bible (show children a Bible).
- But God wants us to talk to him too. That is what we do when we pray. Prayer is talking to God. I can talk to God anywhere and at any time.
- Sometimes I talk to God like I do in Sunday School, with my eyes closed and my hands together. But I don't have to do that to talk to God.
  - I can talk to God when I am running in the park.
  - I can talk to God when I am sitting quietly at home.
  - I can talk to God when I am lying in my bed.
- God always hears me.
- I can whisper (speak quietly) and God hears me.
- I can shout (speak loudly) and God hears me.
- I can think things in my head (point to head) and God hears me.
- I can talk to God about everything.
- God wants me to tell him when I am happy (ask children to make a happy face).
- God wants me to tell him when I am sad (ask the children to make a sad face).
- God wants me to ask him for the things I need, and to thank him for the good things he gives me.
- God wants me to say sorry when I have been naughty.
- God is so big, and so good and so wonderful.
- God is my friend. He wants me to talk to him.

Prayer

Dear God, please help me to talk to you every day. Amen.

Visual aids

- A Bible
- Pictures of children doing different things.

Activities

1. Sing a praise song, eg praise him, praise him, all ye little children.
2. Show children pictures of children doing different things - "Can I pray to God when .....?" Show children pictures of different times of day - "Can I pray to God in the morning?" etc.
3. Give each child a piece of paper with "I can talk to God anytime, anywhere " written on the bottom. Cut out pictures of children doing different things from magazines. Child glues pictures onto sheet of paper.

Reinforcement

1. Bedtime. Talk about the sorts of things for which to say sorry, etc. Encourage child to say a simple prayer. Use one topic at a time.
2. When talking with your child through the day, say "Is that something you could tell God?" Aim is to reinforce that God wants to listen to us.
3. Show child pictures of different times of day – sunrise, breakfast, lunch, afternoon, etc. Ask "Is this the best time to talk to God?" Reinforce that we can talk to God anytime and he always listens.

Term 2 Lesson 12

How do I please God?
~ Obeying ~

Lesson aim: to teach that obedience is pleasing to God

Preparation

1. Read John 14:15,
   1 John 5:3,
   Ephesians 6 v1-4,
   1 Peter 2 v13-14.
2. Answer the following questions :
   ▪ how do we demonstrate our love for God? (John 14:15, 1 John 5:3)
   ▪ whom does God command us to obey? (Ephesians 6:1-4, 1 Peter 2:13-14)
3. Think about the principle of obedience and how it applies in your situation. Think about the children in your care - how can you help them develop habits of obedience?
4. Pray for each child you teach, that God will help those in authority over them to demand obedience.
5. Choose appropriate visual aids.

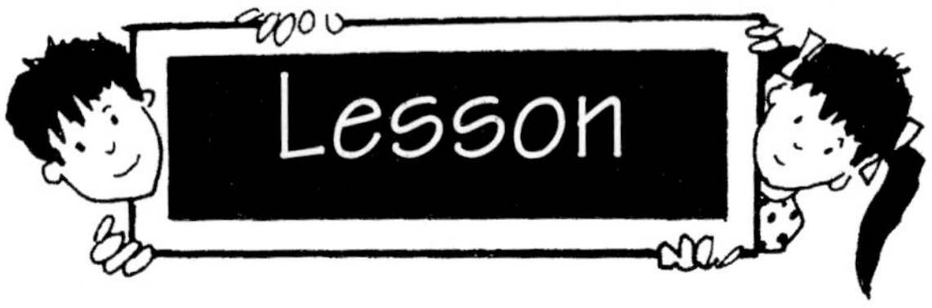

- Use finger puppets (see visual aids) to act out a scene where child is being disobedient.
- Does this made mummy/daddy happy? No, it makes her/him sad.
- Act out a scene where child is being obedient.
- Does this make mummy/daddy happy? Yes, it makes her/him happy.
- When we do what daddy and mummy tell us to it makes God happy as well.
- When Jesus was a little boy he did what his daddy and mummy said - and the Bible tells us that this made God very happy (Luke 2 v51-52).
- God wants us to be like Jesus and do what our daddies and mummies tell us to do.

Prayer

Dear God, please help me to do what daddy and mummy ask me to do. Amen.

Visual aids

- Finger puppets: Make from a piece of paper folded in half, and cut out to fit finger. Sellotape or staple sides together. Draw on a face.

Activities

1. Photocopy page 51, one for 2 children. Cut along cutting line. Fold in half and staple along top and down side to form a hand puppet. Help child draw a smile on one side and a curving down mouth on the other side.
   ▪ Ask children to show you the sad side - talk about disobedience making daddy, mummy and God sad.
   ▪ Ask children to show you the happy side - talk about obedience making daddy, mummy and God happy.
   (If you have no access to a photocopier, fold an A4 sheet of paper in half, and draw the faces on yourself).

2. Play "Simon Says", getting children to do various simple activities. (Don't make children out if they fail to do the activity - wait until all have completed it. If a child refuses to do the activity they must be out. Disobedience has consequences.)

Reinforcement

1. Praise child when he/she is obedient. "Isn't it fun when you do as you're told? It makes everyone happy - daddy, mummy, you and God."
2. When a child needs to be punished, make sure he/she knows why they are being punished, that it makes daddy/mummy/God sad. (**NB** child should be punished for willful disobedience, not childish carelessness).

fold

cut

cut

fold

Term 2 Lesson 13

How do I please God?
~ Helping ~

Lesson aim: To teach that being helpful is pleasing to God

Preparation

1. Read Psalm 121:1-2,
   Hebrews 2:14-18,
   Acts 9:36-43,
   1 Chronicles 28:20-21, Acts 18:27-28,
   2 Corinthians 1:8-11, 2 Chronicles 19:1-3.
2. Answer the following questions:-
   - when I need help, where should I go? (Ps 121)
   - why is Jesus able to help? (Hebrews 12)
   - how can we help other people?
   (Acts 9, 1 Chronicles 28, Acts 18, 2 Corinthians 1)
   - should we help everyone in need? (2 Chron 19)
3. Think about ways you can be a help.
4. Pray for each child you teach, asking God to help you encourage them to be helpers.
5. Choose appropriate visual aids.

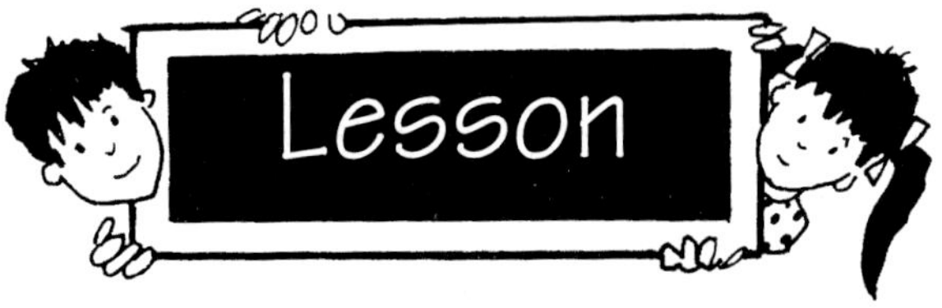

- Remember - small children love to help.
- Start lesson by telling children about Dorcas (Acts 9), helping people because she loved God. Tell them what Dorcas did for people.
- The children cannot help in that way, so talk about the sort of things they can do to be helpful.
  - picking up their toys
  - carrying things for mummy /daddy.
  - giving out crayons at Sunday School
  - passing round drinks,etc.
- Get children to perform the actions as you talk about them.

Prayer

Dear God, please help me to help other people. Amen.

Activities

1. Sort out the Sunday School toys with children helping. This not only reinforces helping but is also educational in encouraging child to differentiate between different categories. Praise children for helping. Point out that helping makes you pleased and makes God pleased.
2. A "helping " pendant: Photocopy page 53 onto coloured card - one for every 2 children, and page 54 onto white paper for each child.
   - Prior to lesson, cut out circles of card and punch a hole at X.
   - Cut out 2 circles, then glue them one on each side of circle of coloured card.
   - Thread a length of wool through the hole so that the card circle can hang round the child's neck. (make sure the wool is easily broken – danger of strangulation!)
   - Ask child to do something to be helpful then put the pendant round child's neck as a badge of helpfulness.
   - This can be made using cut outs from magazines if preferred.
3. Ask children to help put things away at the end of Sunday School, e.g. the chair they sit on, toys into boxes. Praise them for being helpful.

Reinforcement

1. Ask child to help you tidy up toys etc. at end of each day. Praise child for being helpful. Point out that it makes you happy and God happy.
2. Allow child to "help" (This can be time-consuming). Do not reject offers of help unless there is a safety hazard.
3. Encourage child to have a regular chore, eg emptying waste paper baskets.

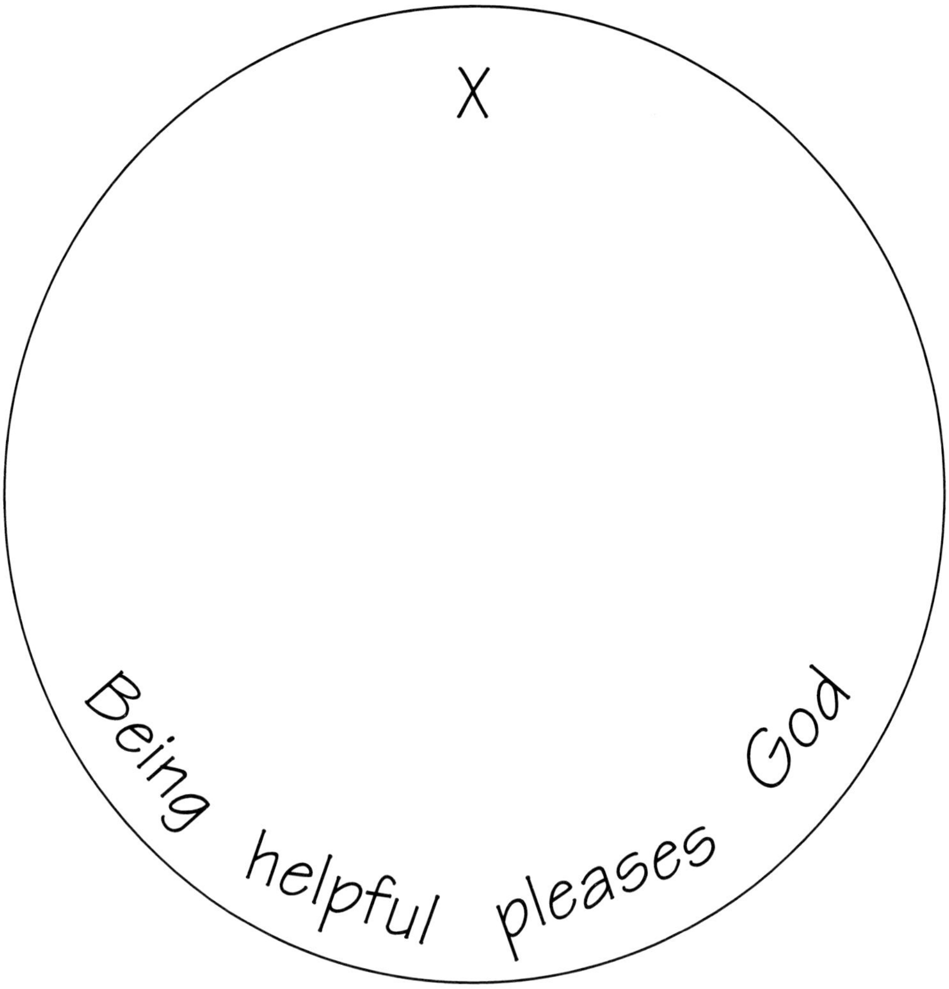
X
Being helpful pleases God

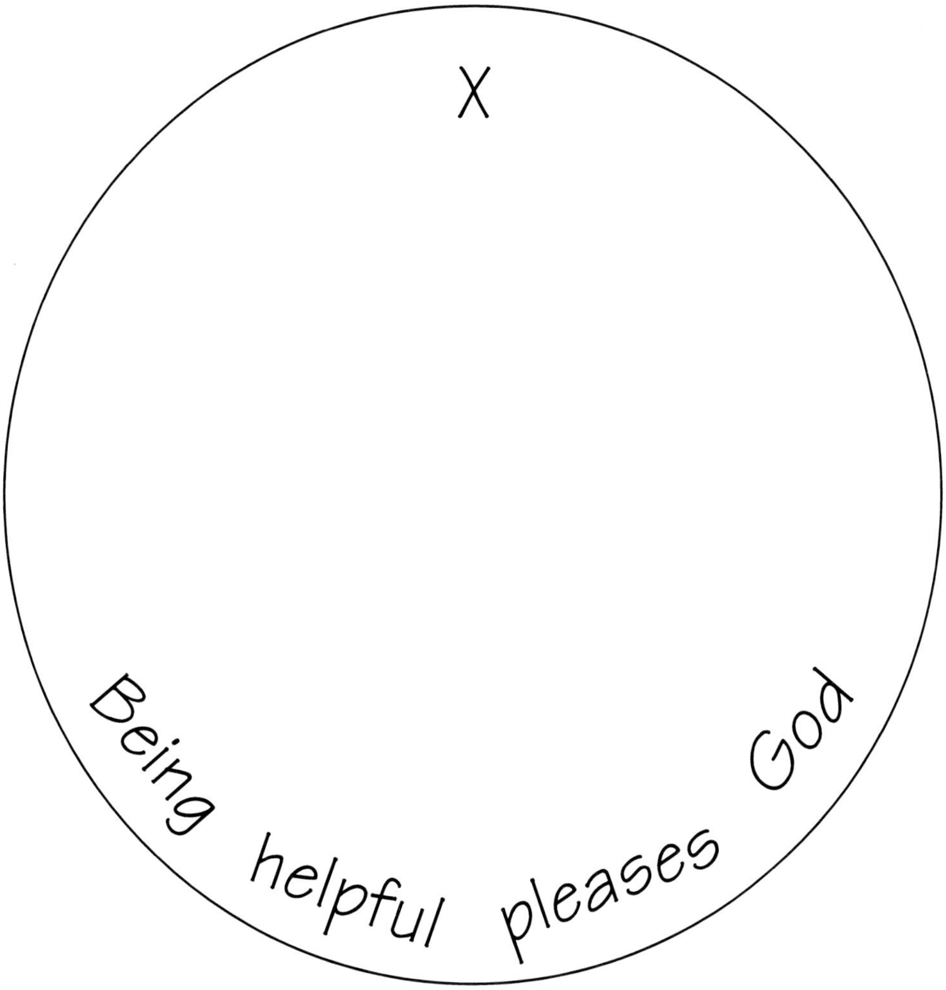
X
Being helpful pleases God

Term 2 Lesson 14

How do I please God?
~ Thanking ~

Lesson aim: to teach the children to say thank you to God for the good things he gives them

Preparation

1. Read Psalm 50:22-23, Colossians 2:6-7, Hebrews 12:28, Colossians 3:15-17; 4:2, 1 Chronicles 16:34-36, Psalm 118:21, Matthew 14:18-19, 1 Corinthians 1:4; 15:55-57, 1 Thessalonians 5:16-18.
2. Answer the following question:-
   - why should I be thankful? (Psalm 50, Colossians2, Hebrews 12)
   - when should I be thankful? Colossians 3:15-17; 4:2
   - for what should I be thankful? (1 Chronicles 16, Psalm 118, Matthew 14, 1 Corinthians 1:4; 15:55-57, 1 Thessalonians 5)
3. Think about the times you are thankful. Look back over the past week – how many times have you complained about something?
4. Pray for each child you teach, asking God to encourage them to be thankful.
5. Choose appropriate visual aids.

- Have something small to hand to each child (eg

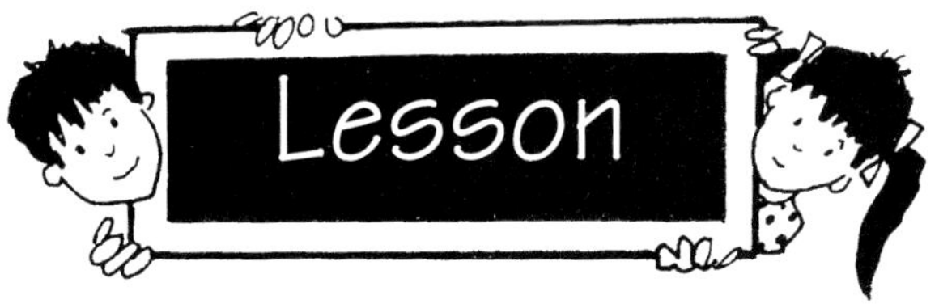

smarties, a plain biscuit). As you give it, get the child to say "thank-you". Talk about why we say "thank you" - we are showing how happy we are to get that thing. Put up pictures of the sorts of things that the children will thank God for.
- food
- family
- friends

Prayer

A short prayer thanking God for something.

Visual aids

Pictures of things for which to thank God.

Activities

1. Thank you book: Photocopy pages 56 and 57 back to back on coloured paper for each child. Cut along centre line, put 2 halves together and fold in half to make a book. Staple at fold line.
   - Pages read: Thank you God for ...., the sun, the rain, flowers, birds, food, my family, and friends.
   - (Alternatively, use a sheet of A4 coloured paper and copy details from pages 56 and 57)
   - Each child will also need a yellow circle of gummed paper for the sun, pictures of birds, flowers, food cut from magazines, and a picture of a family and of children playing (page 58)
   - Children glue cut outs onto pages and draw rain drops coming down from the cloud.
2. Make a chain of the children. Pass items down the line with each child saying 'thank you' as the item is passed to him/her.

Reinforcement

1. Saying thank you to God at meal times.
2. Thank you prayers at bed time.
3. Encouraging child to say thank you for items received.
4. Make a collage using pictures cut from magazines of all the things we can thank God for.
5. Go for a walk. Use the time to identify all the things that God has made. Thank God for them.

flowers

birds

Thank you
God for...

friends

the rain

food

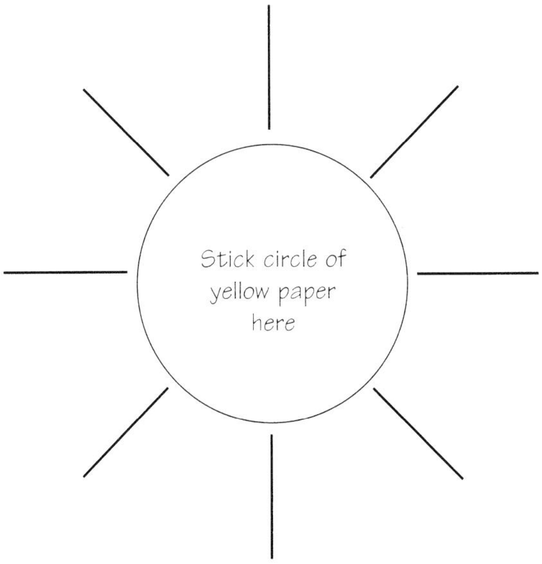

the sun

my family

If you prefer, use cutouts of adult figures and children playing from magazines

Term 2 Lesson 15

How do I please God?
~ Being kind ~

Lesson aim: to teach that being kind to other people is pleasing to God

Preparation

1. Read Luke 10:25-37.
2. Answer the following questions:
   ▪ what is required by the law in order to inherit eternal life?
   ▪ can I keep the law?
   ▪ why was it so shocking to Jesus' hearers for a Samaritan to have pity on a Jew?
   ▪ who is my neighbour?
3. Think about good deeds. Are they the path to acceptance with God, or the necessary fruits that come from a relationship with God? (Read John 3:16, James 2 v14-19)
4. Pray for each child you teach, asking God to help him/her learn to be kind.
5. Choose appropriate visual aids.

- Show children a picture of a family. Point out the daddy, mummy, etc. and that this is called a family.
- We are part of God's family. God is our father. Sometimes grown ups say, "dear heavenly father" when they pray to God.
- God loves each one of us very much. He has told us in the Bible what we should do to please him.
- When we are kind we please God. Jesus told a story about being kind.
- A man was going on a long journey. Suddenly some bad people jumped out on him and hit him and stole his clothes and his money. They left him lying badly hurt on the side of the road. That wasn't being kind, was it?
- Later on a man walked by. He didn't stop to help the man who was hurt. Was that being kind? No.
- Then another man came along. He went over and looked at the man who was hurt. Perhaps he was going to help him. No. He, too, walked on.
- Finally a third man came along. He also saw the hurt man lying by the side of the road. Straight away he went to him and cleaned the sore places and bandaged them. Then he put the man on his donkey and took him and cared for him till he was better.
- Which one was the kind man? The man who looked after the man who was hurt.
- God wants us to be like the kind man.
- God doesn't want us to hit our friends or our brothers and sisters - because that isn't being kind.
- God doesn't want us to punch or bite our friends or our brothers and sisters - because that isn't being kind.
- God wants us to comfort (look after, cuddle, make happy again) our friends or our brothers and sisters when they are sad, because that is being kind.
- And God wants us to share our toys with our friends and our brothers and sisters - because that is being kind.
- When we are kind, we make God happy.

Prayer

Dear God, please help me to be kind. Amen.

Visual aids

- Pictures of a family.
- children doing kind things.
- Child's Story Bible for pictures of Good Samaritan.

Activities

1. Practice sharing. Have a pile of bricks /duplo on the table. Share them out, getting children to hand them round. Do the same with plain biscuits (make sure there are only half the number of biscuits). There are not enough biscuits to go round. Do some children miss out? No, we share the biscuits (break each biscuit in half and hand out).
   ▪ Put one toy on the table. Not enough to go round, cannot be broken up. Take it in turns.
2. Hold up pictures of children doing kind/unkind things. Ask "Is this being kind?" God likes us to be kind.

Reinforcement

1. Make a collage using pictures of children being kind cut from magazines. Write "God is pleased when I am kind".
2. Praise children when he/she does kind things. Reinforce - God is happy when you are kind.

Term 2 Lesson 16

How do I please God?
~ Saying sorry ~

Lesson aim: to show the need to say sorry when I do something wrong

Preparation

1. Read Matthew 6:9-15, Luke 17:3-4, Acts 17:30.
2. Answer the following questions:
   - why should I forgive someone who says sorry?
   - can I be put right with God if I do not repent?
3. Think about my position in God's sight. Is there anything I have not repented of.
4. Pray for each child you teach that God will help him/her to be truly sorry for wrong doing.
5. Choose appropriate visual aids.

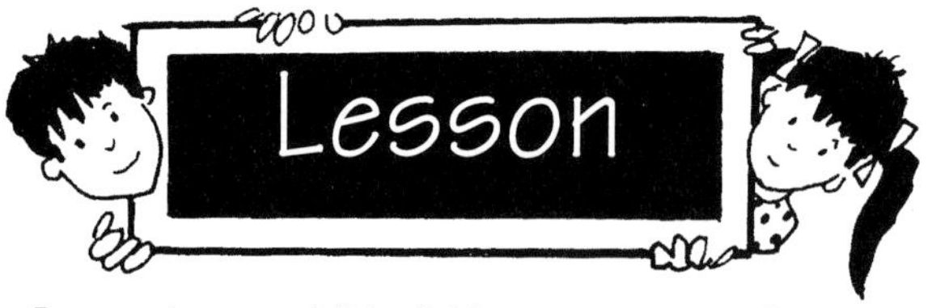

- Remember - a child of this age cannot differentiate between deliberate naughtiness and childish carelessness. The examples you use should be things that the child needs to say sorry for, not necessarily things that require punishment (deliberate disobedience).
- Introduction: Talk about the children's day; encourage them to tell you their sequence of daily events eg I get up in the morning - do you? Do Mummy and Daddy come and help you to get out of bed? Do you get dressed etc. Begin with daily activities dressing / washing / drinking / eating.
- Discuss other things they may do in the day - go to the shops with Mummy / help to do the washing of dishes or clothes.
- Lesson: Do you ever do anything that makes your Mummy / Daddy say "NO , don't do that!" or "NO, STOP it!"?
- Discuss the sort of things that might be:
  - spilling drink / food
  - dropping plates
  - climbing on the table
  - snatching another child's toy
  - hitting another child
  - pinching
  - hair pulling
  - running across the road.
- Do you ever say "sorry"? It's kind to say "sorry" for:
  - breaking things
  - taking things
  - hitting people
  - hurting people
  - saying nasty things to people
- Suppose someone has done something to you that you don't like - it is a good thing if they say "sorry" to you. Mummy is pleased if you say "sorry" to her if you have done something wrong.

Prayer

Dear Jesus, please help me to say "sorry" if I do something wrong. Amen.

Visual aids

Pictures of children doing naughty and careless things

Activities

1. See page 61. Photocopy for each child. Cut out circles and glue either side of a cardboard template. Child can glue pieces of material onto clothing of pictures or colour.
2. Encourage children to say sorry if you spot them doing wrong things.

Reinforcement

Notes for Parents.

1. Think through why we need forgiveness. Is saying sorry, the same as asking for forgiveness?
2. To whom should we say sorry? God? the person we have wronged?
3. Is there any point in saying sorry if I don't mean it?
4. When do I say sorry? At the time of the offence if possible. The longer you leave it, the harder it gets.
5. Remind your child to say sorry when he/she does something wrong. Remind them that this pleases God.
6. Pray with your child, thanking God for forgiveness.

Cut out circles for children to colour.
Stick one on each side of a circle of card with a lollipop stick handle, or use the handle shape on the left-hand side as a template.

Term 2 Lesson 17

How do I please God? ~ Praising God ~

Lesson aim: to show how we can praise God

Preparation

1. Read Psalms 145 and 150
2. Answer the following questions:
   - what are the reasons given for praising God?
   - who should praise God?
   - how should we praise God?
3. Think back over the last week. What can I praise God for?
4. Pray for each child you teach, that he/she will grow up to praise God for all his goodness to him/her.
5. Choose appropriate visual aids.

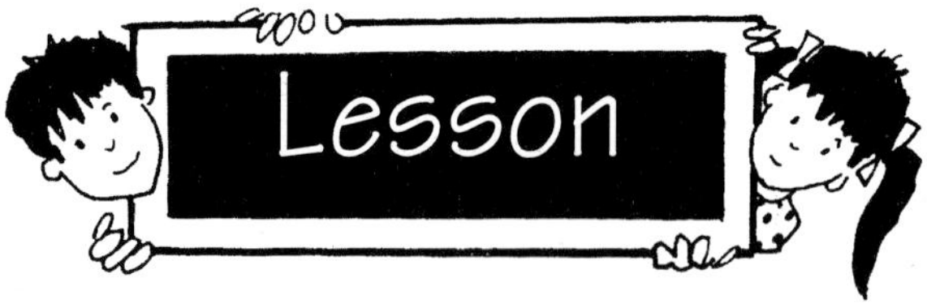

- Introduction: Try to find out from the children the sort of things they enjoy doing - running, jumping, singing, dancing, making a noise, shouting, banging, swimming.
- What do we look like when we are happy? Practice pulling a smiling face in a mirror. How can you tell if your Mummy is happy - does she sing? Sometimes you can hear a man walking along the street whistling - do you think he might be happy?
- What does a cat do when it is happy? Purrs - all make purring noises - and a dog? (Wags his tail).
- Lesson: When we came to church this morning we all stood up and sang together, didn't we? That is because we are happy and are singing to God and telling him that we think he is a wonderful God and thanking him for all the lovely things he gives to us. Things like - refer back to appropriate things that children had mentioned make them happy. One of the ways we can please God is to sing to him and make a happy noise and dance - let's do that now.
- Sing a praise song such as "Clap your hands all you people" - the chorus only - children can "dance" at the same time and clap their hands.

Visual aids

- Cassette recorder and music
- Pictures of cat and dog
- Pictures of children dancing, adults in church.

Activities

1. Make a "musical instrument". Each child requires a yoghurt pot or toilet roll core, rice/macaroni/dried peas, a piece of colourful wrapping paper.
   - If using toilet roll core seal one end prior to lesson.
   - Children place rice/macaroni/dried peas into container.
   - Cover with cling film. Child glues piece of wrapping paper round container.
   - Once all musical instruments are made sing the praise song again.
2. Make a badge for each child.
   - Each child requires a circle of coloured card with a safety pin taped to the back. Prior to lesson draw 2 eyes. Child draws happy mouth.
   - Remind child that God is pleased when we praise him.

Reinforcement

1. Either go for a walk, go into the garden, or use picture books. Identify the various good things God has done. Ask "Who made the flowers?" etc. "How can we thank God? By praising him".
2. Praise your child when he/she does something good. Ask - does it make you happy when I praise you? Talk about God being happy when we praise him.

Christmas Story 1

The Birth of Jesus

Lesson aim: to teach that Jesus is the Son of God

Preparation

1. Read Luke 2:1-7
2. Answer the following questions:-
   - how do we know from this passage that the birth of Jesus was a historical fact and not a myth?
   - why did Joseph and Mary travel from Nazareth to Bethlehem?
   - why was it important for Jesus to be born on Bethlehem? (see Micah 5:2)
   - do you know how babies were wrapped? A piece of cloth was laid on a flat surface and one of the corners was turned down. The baby was placed on the cloth so that head was towards turned down corner, and feet towards point c. With the baby's arms by the side of his body, point b was wrapped across the baby Then point c was pulled up and secured by wrapping point a. across the baby. The whole thing was secured by wrapping strips of cloth around the baby.

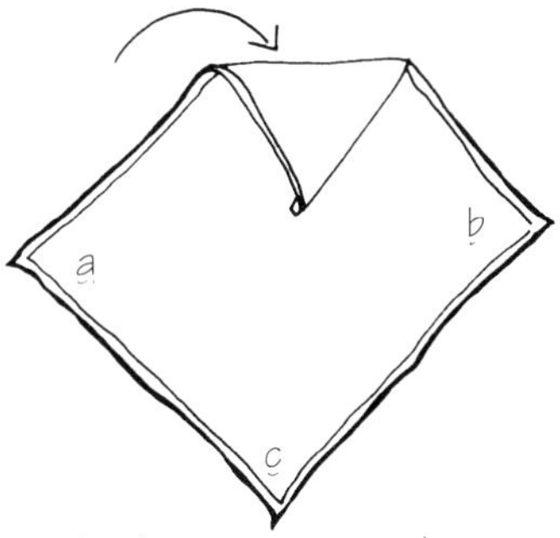

3. Think about the wonder of God becoming man.
4. Pray for each child you teach, asking God to help you tell the story simply and truthfully.
5. Choose appropriate visual aids.

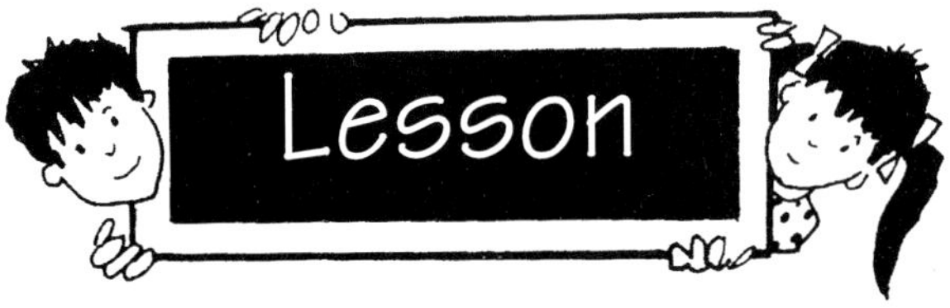

- It will soon be Christmas. Christmas is the time when we are very happy and give each other presents. This is because we are remembering someone's birthday. At Christmas we remember when a very special baby boy was born. His name was Jesus, and he was not like any of us. He had a mummy, just like we do, and his mummy's name was Mary. But his daddy wasn't like our daddies. Jesus' daddy was God. Mary had a husband and his name was Joseph. One day Joseph and Mary had to go on a long journey to a town called Bethlehem. The journey took a long, long time and it was very late when they got to Bethlehem. Mary was very tired. Joseph went to the inn and said: "can we stay here?" The innkeeper said, "No , my house is full up. There is no room for you." What could they do? Mary was very tired and her baby was going to be born. The innkeeper was sorry for Mary. He said they could stay in the stable where the animals lived.
- So Joseph took Mary to the stable. There the baby Jesus was born. Mary wrapped him up to keep him warm, but there was no bed for him. So she made a bed in the straw in the animals' feed box, and the baby Jesus slept there.

Visual aids

- Either pictures from a Child's Story Bible or models.
- Young children like to play with the models, so make sure they are not breakable. The crib scene will be built up over the 3 stories, with different figures added each time. A commercial crib set can be used or you can make your own using a cardboard box for the stable and paper cups/yoghurt pots and egg cartons for the figures. (see page 64). It is helpful to have a baby doll to show the children how the baby was wrapped up, and a box of straw to put the baby in.

Activities

1. Dress up the children and let them act out the story.
2. Photocopy bottom half of page 64 onto dark coloured paper – 1 for each child. Prior to lesson cut out 3 figures and the stable outline. Give each child a sheet of white/ light coloured A4 paper with "Jesus is the Son of God " written along the bottom of one of the long sides. Child glues stable outline in place, then glues 3 figures in the middle to make a picture.
3. Sing "Away in a manger" - first verse only.

Story Aid: The Birth of Jesus

A cardboard box for the stable, decorated with straw (Shredded Wheat or crepe paper), some plastic animals, cardboard trough etc. Perhaps the children could make plasticine animals. Cut some windows out of the side and draw wooden planking round the inside.

Figures can be made from paper cups and sections of egg carton. Sellotape the egg carton onto the paper cup. Draw a face on and some clothes. "Dress" with a piece of material tied around the middle with wool.

Reinforcement

1. Wrap up a small figure. (e.g. Playmobil or Fisher Price) in a strip of cloth. Show it to child, then "hide" it in a stable like building. (You can put toy animals there as well). Tell child you are going to find the baby Jesus. Look in the various places - e.g. Fisher-Price School house, dolls house, farm, firestation. etc. Ask each time, "Was Jesus in the .....?" Once Jesus has been found, retell the story.
2. Use a commercial crib set to go over the story. Allow child to move the figures around to tell you the story. Ask, "Why was baby Jesus so special?" "Because he is God".

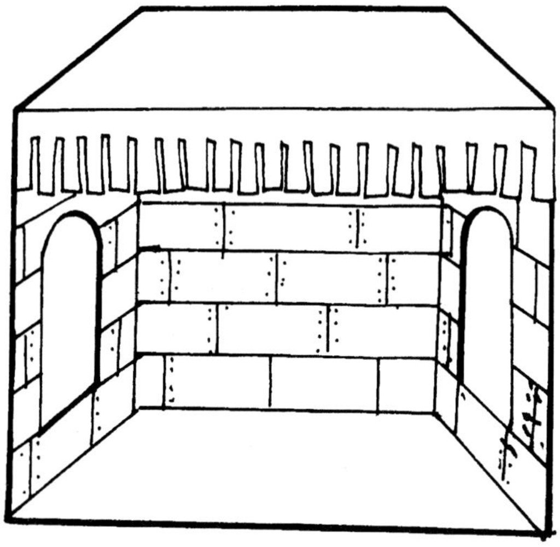

Christmas Story 2

The Shepherds

Lesson aim: to teach that Jesus is the Son of God

Preparation

1 .Read Luke 2 v8-20.
2. Answer the following questions:-
   - why were the shepherds given proof that Jesus was the expected Messiah?
   - is peace on earth for everyone?
   - who are the people with whom God is pleased?
3. Think about the wonder of God becoming man.
4. Pray for each child you teach, asking God to help you tell the story simply and truthfully.
5. Choose appropriate visual aids.

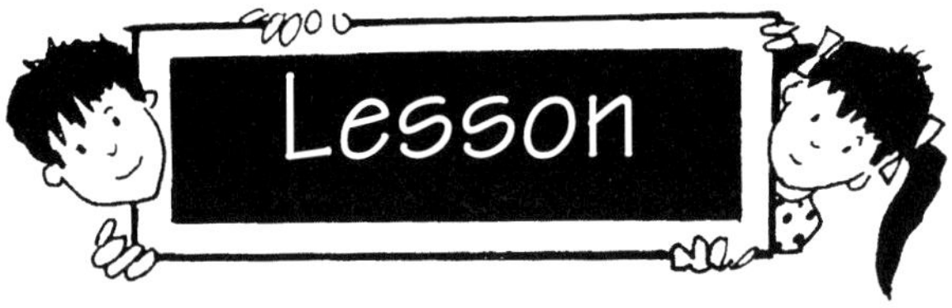

- Remind the children of previous lesson - the birth of Jesus - using the crib scene already set up.
- On the night that Jesus was born some shepherds were in a field, looking after their sheep. Suddenly an angel appeared and a bright light shone all round them. The shepherds were very, very frightened. The angel said, "Don't be afraid. I've come to give you good news". Then the angel told them all about the special baby who had been born in Bethlehem and how he was God.
- Then a lot of angels appeared, all singing songs about God.
- After the angels had gone back to heaven the shepherds said, "Let's go to Bethlehem and see this special baby". They hurried off and found Mary and Joseph, and the baby Jesus lying in the animals' feed box, just as the angel had told them.

Visual aids

See notes for Christmas Story 1.

Activities

1. Dress up children and act out the story.
2. Make a Christmas card for each child. Children decorate card. (See page 66)
   - Or, using old Christmas cards cut out scenes and allow children to glue them onto pieces of card. Inside write : to .... (ask child what to write) Happy Christmas, with love from ....
3. Sing "Away in a manger".

Reinforcement

1.Ask child - "how do we send messages?"
(a) Write a letter/note - write a short note to a member of the family asking them to bring something, eg soft toy, biscuit. Send the note by the child, asking them to bring back the requested item.
(b) Telephone - use real or toy telephone to phone and pass on a message.
(c) Send a message through another person - ask child to ask some other person for ....
   - When God wanted to send a special message what did he use? Retell the story. Point out that only God sends messages through angels.

2. Ask child, what do shepherds do? Child pretends to be a shepherd and collects all his/her sheep (soft toys etc). Put the sheep inside a sheepfold (made from cushions, toy boxes etc). Shepherd sits down an guard. Retell the story.
   - Reinforce "Jesus was special because he is God".
3. Make some Christmas biscuits - use star shapes, angels, etc.

Christmas Cookies

8oz flour, 4.5oz margarine, 4oz soft brown sugar
1 teaspoon ground ginger, 2oz black treacle,
2oz golden syrup

Combine all ingredients in a bowl and knead until evenly coloured. Roll out on a floured surface and cut into decorative shapes. Make a hole in the centre with a skewer, then bake at 375 F for 20 mins. Decorate with coloured glace icing, silver balls, sugar flowers etc.

4. Use Christmas preparations to reinforce the fact that Jesus is God. "We are doing all these things because ......"

They saw the baby
lying in the manger

Luke 2:16

Christmas Story 3

The Wise Men

Lesson aim: to teach that Jesus is the Son of God

Teacher Preparation

1. Read Matthew 2:1-12.
2. Answer the following question:
   - how many men were there?
   - why did they go to Herod initially?
   - did Herod understand who the wise men were looking for?
   - where was Jesus when the wise men found him? (Matthew 2:11)
3. Think about the journey the wise men would have had, and their determination to find the special baby.
4. Pray for each child, asking God to help you get over the fact that this special baby was God.
5. Choose appropriate visual aids.

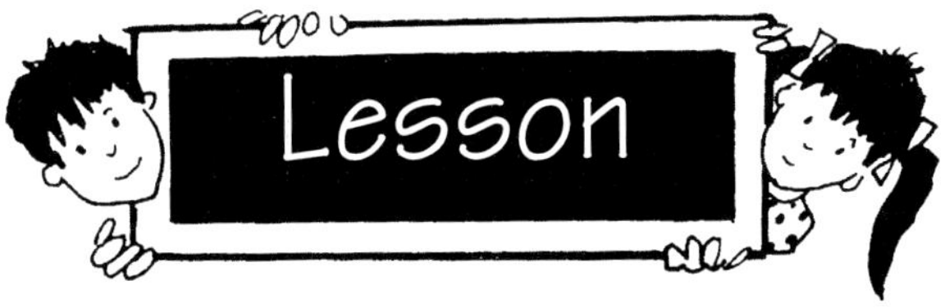

- Using the visual aids from previous 2 weeks, remind children of the birth of Jesus and the shepherds being told about him.
- When Jesus was born a new star appeared in the sky. Some wise men saw this star and knew that it meant a very special baby had been born.They decided to go and find this baby and give him presents.
- First of all they went to the King. "We have come to see the special baby", they said. Do you think the King knew where the baby Jesus was? No.
- But some of the King's teachers knew that God's word said a very special baby would be born at Bethlehem. He was God's Son.
- So the wise men set off for Bethlehem. Imagine how excited they were when they saw the new star going in front of them. At last the star stopped moving. It was right over the place where the baby Jesus was. The wise men went in to see the baby Jesus, and they gave him the presents.

Visual aids

- As for Christmas Story 1. NB by the time the wise men came to Jesus the family had moved from the stable and were living in a house.

Activities

1. Dress up the children and act out story.
2. Photocopy page 68 for each child on card. Fold along fold line. Cut around thick black line and fold 2 bottom flaps. Child colours figure or glues on scraps of material. Glue bottom flaps together so that wise man on camel is standing up.
3. Play "Pass the parcel". Make a tinsel star for each child and wrap up the parcel so that one star is obtained for every layer of paper removed. Make sure that each child gets a star. At the end ask, "Who brought presents to Jesus?" "Why did they bring presents to Jesus? "Why was Jesus a special baby?" (If you have a large class of children you may want to do this in small groups.)

Reinforcement

1. Make sure your child knows what a star looks like. Look at the night sky and find a star. Try and find the brightest star in the sky. Go over the story.
2. When opening Christmas presents remind child: who brought presents to Jesus? Why did the wise men bring presents to Jesus? etc.

fold

We have come to
worship him
Matthew 2:2

Cut around thick black line only

fold

fold